The Worship of the Generative Powers

A History of Phallic Worship
by Thomas Wright

Fredonia Books
Amsterdam, The Netherlands

The Worship of the Generative
Powers
A History of Phallic Worship

by
Thomas Wright

ISBN 1-58963-037-8

Reprinted from the 1992 edition

Fredonia Books
Amsterdam, The Netherlands
http://www.FredoniaBooks.com

THE WORSHIP OF THE
GENERATIVE POWERS

DURING THE MIDDLE AGES
OF WESTERN EUROPE

BY

THOMAS WRIGHT

WITH PLATES

Fig 1.

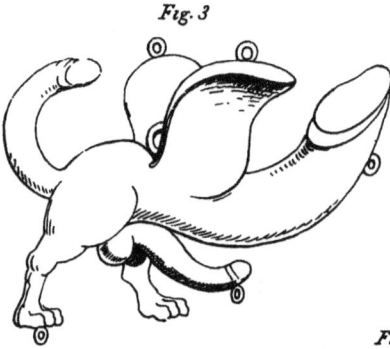

Fig. 3

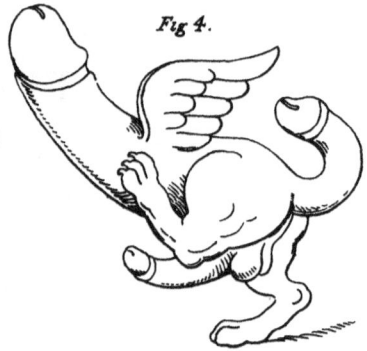

Fig 4.

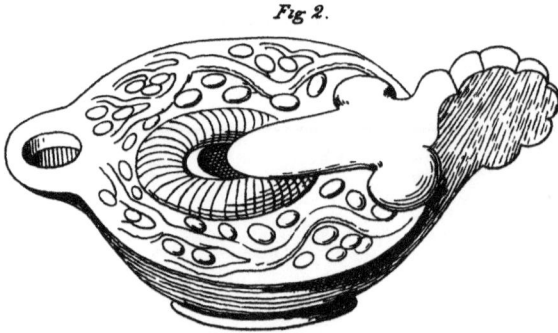

Fig 2.

PLATE I

EX VOTI OF WAX, FROM ISERNIA

THE WORSHIP OF THE GENERATIVE POWERS DURING THE MIDDLE AGES OF WESTERN EUROPE

RICHARD PAYNE KNIGHT has written with great learning on the origin and history of the worship of Priapus among the ancients. This worship, which was but a part of that of the generative powers, appears to have been the most ancient of the superstitions of the human race,[1] has prevailed more or less among all known peoples before the introduction of Christianity, and, singularly enough, so deeply it seems to have been implanted in human nature, that even the promulgation of the Gospel did not abolish it, for it continued to exist, accepted and often encouraged by the mediæval clergy. The occasion of Payne Knight's work was the discovery that

---

[1] There appears to be a chance of this worship being claimed for a very early period in the history of the human race. It has been recently stated in the " Moniteur," that, in the province of Venice, in Italy, excavations in a bone-cave have brought to light, beneath ten feet of stalagmite, bones of animals, mostly postertiary, of the usual description found in such places, flint implements, with a needle of bone having an eye and point, and a plate of an argillaceous compound, on which was scratched a rude drawing of a phallus.—*Moniteur*, Jan. 1865.

this worship continued to prevail in his time, in a very remarkable form, at Isernia in the kingdom of Naples, a full description of which will be found in his work. The town of Isernia was destroyed, with a great portion of its inhabitants, in the terrible earthquake which so fearfully devastated the kingdom of Naples on the 26th of July, 1805, nineteen years after the appearance of the book alluded to. Perhaps with it perished the last trace of the worship of Priapus in this particular form; but Payne Knight was not acquainted with the fact that this superstition, in a variety of forms, prevailed throughout Southern and Western Europe largely during the Middle Ages, and that in some parts it is hardly extinct at the present day; and, as its effects were felt to a more considerable extent than people in general suppose in the most intimate and important relations of society, whatever we can do to throw light upon its mediæval existence, though not an agreeable subject, cannot but form an important and valuable contribution to the better knowledge of mediæval history. Many interesting facts relating to this subject were brought together in a volume published in Paris by Monsieur J. A. Dulaure, under the title, *Des Divinités Génératices chez les Anciens et les Modernes*, forming part of an *Histoire Abrégée des dif-*

férens Cultes, by the same author.[1] This book, however, is still very imperfect; and it is the design of the following pages to give, with the most interesting of the facts already collected by Dulaure, other facts and a description and explanation of monuments, which tend to throw a greater and more general light on this curious subject.

The mediæval worship of the generative powers, represented by the generative organs, was derived from two distinct sources. In the first place, Rome invariably carried into the provinces she had conquered her own institutions and forms of worship, and established them permanently. In exploring the antiquities of these provinces, we are astonished at the abundant monuments of the worship of Priapus in all the shapes and with all the attributes and accompaniments, with which we are already so well acquainted in Rome and Italy. Among the remains of Roman civilization in Gaul, we find statues or statuettes of Priapus, altars dedicated to him, the gardens and fields entrusted to his care, and the phallus, or male member, figured in a variety of shapes as a protecting power against evil influences of various kinds. With this idea the well-known figure was sculptured on the walls of public build-

[1] The second edition of this work, published in 1825, is by much the best, and is considerably enlarged from the first.

ings, placed in conspicuous places in the interior of the house, worn as an ornament by women, and suspended as an amulet to the necks of children. Erotic scenes of the most extravagant description covered vessels of metal, earthenware, and glass, intended, on doubt, for festivals and usages more or less connected with the worship of the principle of fecundity.

At Aix in Provence there was found, on or near the site of the ancient baths, to which it had no doubt some relation, an enormous phallus, encircled with garlands, sculptured in white marble. At Le Chatelet, in Champagne, on the site of a Roman town, a colossal phallus was also found. Similar objects in bronze, and of smaller dimensions, are so common, that explorations are seldom carried on upon a Roman site in which they are not found, and examples of such objects abound in the museums, public or private, of Roman antiquities. The phallic worship appears to have flourished especially at Nemausus, now represented by the city of Nîmes in the south of France, where the symbol of this worship appeared in sculpture on the walls of its amphitheatre and on other buildings, in forms some of which we can hardly help regarding as fanciful, or even playful. Some of the more remarkable of these are figured in our plates, II and III.

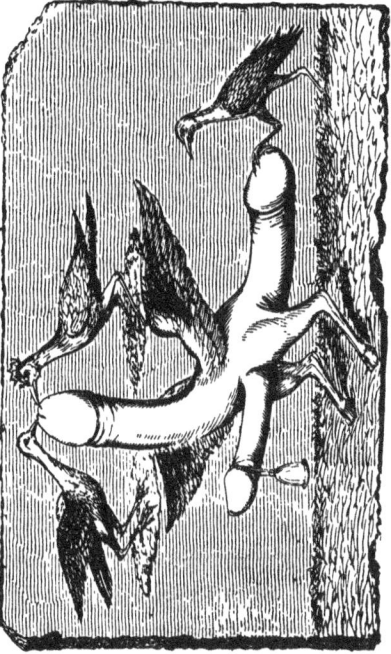

Fig. 2.

Fig. 4.

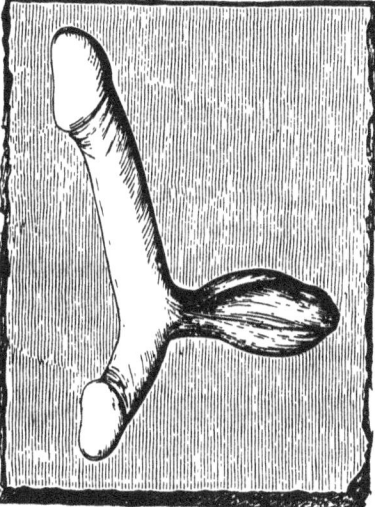

Fig. 1.

Fig. 3.

PLATE II
ROMAN SCULPTURES FROM NIMES

The first of these,[1] is the figure of a double phallus. It is sculptured on the lintel of one of the vomitories, or issues, of the second range of seats of the Roman amphitheatre, near the entrance-gate which looks to the south. The double and the triple phallus are very common among the small Roman bronzes, which appear to have served as amulets and for other similar purposes. In the latter, one phallus usually serves as the body, and is furnished with legs, generally those of the goat; a second occupies the usual place of this organ; and a third appears in that of a tail. On a pilaster of the amphitheatre of Nîmes we see a triple phallus of this description,[2] with goat's legs and feet. A small bell is suspended to the smaller phallus in front; and the larger organ which forms the body is furnished with wings. The picture is completed by the introduction of three birds, two of which are pecking the unveiled head of the principal phallus, while the third is holding down the tail with its foot.

Several examples of these triple phalli occur in the *Musée Secret* of the antiquities of Herculaneum and Pompeii. In the examples figured in that work, the hind part of the main phallus assumes clearly

---

[1] Plate ɪɪ, Fig. 1.

[2] See our Plate ɪɪ, Fig. 2.

---

the form of a dog; [1] and to most of them are attached small bells, the explanation of which appears as yet to be very unsatisfactory. The wings also are common attributes of the phallus in these monuments. Plutarch is quoted as an authority for the explanation of the triple phallus as intended to signify multiplication of its productive faculty. [2]

On the top of another pilaster of the amphitheatre at Nîmes, to the right of the principal western entrance, was a bas-relief, also representing a triple phallus, with legs of dog, and winged, but with a further accompaniment. [3] A female, dressed in the Roman stola, stands upon the phallus forming the tail, and holds both it and the one forming the body with a bridle. [4] This bas-relief was taken down in 1829, and is now preserved in the museum of Nîmes.

A still more remarkable monument of this class was found in the course of excavations made at

---

[1] The writer of the text to the *Musée Secret* supposes that this circumstance has some reference to the double meaning given to the Greek word χύων, which was used for the generative organ.

[2] See Auguste Pelet, *Catalogue du Musée de Nîmes*.

[3] Plate II, Fig. 3.

[4] A French antiquary has given an emblematical interpretation of this figure. " Perhaps," he says, " it signifies the empire of woman extending over the three ages of man; on youth, characterized by the bell; on the age of vigour, the ardour of which she restrains; and on old age, which she sustains." This is perhaps more ingenious than convincing.

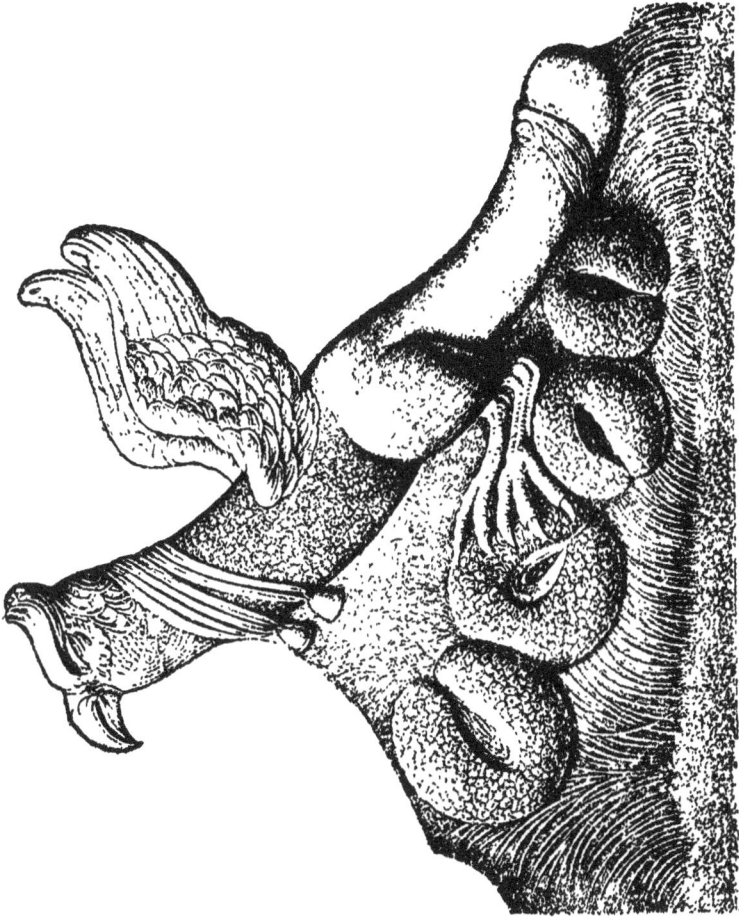

PLATE III

MONUMENT FOUND AT NIMES IN 1825

Nîmes in 1825. It is engraved in our plate xxvi, and
represents a bird, apparently intended for a vulture,
with spread wings and phallic tail, sitting on four
eggs, each of which is designed, no doubt, to represent the female organ. The local antiquarians give to
this, as to the other similar objects, an emblematical
signification; but it may perhaps be more rightly
regarded as a playful conception of the imagination.
A similar design, with some modifications, occurs not
unfrequently among Gallo-Roman antiquities. We
have engraved a figure of the triple phallus governed,
or guided, by the female,[1] from a small bronze plate,
on which it appears in bas-relief; it is now preserved
in a private collection in London, with a duplicate,
which appears to have been cast from the same
mould, though the plate is cut through, and they were
evidently intended for suspension from the neck.
Both came from the collection of M. Baudot of Dijon.
The lady here bridles only the principal phallus; the
legs are, as in the monument last described, those of
a bird, and it is standing upon three eggs, apple-
formed, and representing the organ of the other sex.

In regard to this last-mentioned object, another
very remarkable monument of what appears at
Nîmes to have been by no means a secret worship,

[1] See our Plate III, Fig. 3.

was found there during some excavations on the site of the Roman baths. It is a squared mass of stone, the four sides of which, like the one represented in our engraving, are covered with similar figures of the sexual characteristics of the female, arranged in rows.[1] It has evidently served as a base, probably to a statue, or possibly to an altar. This curious monument is now preserved in the museum at Nîmes.

As Nîmes was evidently a centre of this Priapic worship in the south of Gaul, so there appear to have been, perhaps lesser, centres in other parts, and we may trace it to the northern extremities of the Roman province, even to the other side of the Rhine. On the site of Roman settlements near Xanten, in lower Hesse, a large quantity of pottery and other objects have been found, of a character to leave no doubt as to the prevalence of this worship in that quarter.[2] But the Roman settlement which occupied the site of the modern city of Antwerp appears to have been one of the most remarkable seats of the worship of

[1] See Plate II, Fig. 4.

[2] Two Roman towns, Castra Vetera and Colonia Trajana, stood within no great distance of Xanten, and Ph. Houben, a "notarius" of this town, formed a private museum of antiquities found there, and in 1839, published engravings of them, with a text by Dr. Franz Fiedler. The erotic objects form a separate work under the title, *Antike erotische Bildwerke in Houbens Antiquarium zu Xanten.*

Priapus in the north of Gaul, and it continued to exist there till a comparatively modern period.

When we cross over to Britain we find this worship established no less firmly and extensively in that island. Statuettes of Priapus, phallic bronzes, pottery covered with obscene pictures, are found wherever there are any extensive remains of Roman occupation, as our antiquaries know well. The numerous phallic figures in bronze, found in England, are perfectly identical in character with those which occur in France and Italy. In illustration of this fact, we give two examples of the triple phallus, which appears to have been, perhaps in accordance with the explanation given by Plutarch, an amulet in great favour. The first was found in London in 1842.[1] As in the examples found on the continent, a principal phallus forms the body, having the hinder parts of apparently a dog, with wings of a peculiar form, perhaps intended for those of a dragon. Several small rings are attached, no doubt for the purpose of suspending bells. Our second example [2] was found at York in 1844. It displays a peculiarity of action which, in this case at least, leaves no doubt that the hinder parts were intended to be those of a dog. All antiquaries of any experience know the great num-

[1] See Plate I, Fig. 3.
[2] Plate I, Fig. 4.

ber of obscene subjects which are met with among the fine red pottery which is termed Samian ware, found so abundantly in all Roman sites in our island. They represent erotic scenes in every sense of the word, promiscuous intercourse between the sexes, even vices contrary to nature, with figures of Priapus, and phallic emblems. We give as an example one of the *less* exceptional scenes of this description, copied from a Samian bowl found in Cannon Street, London, in 1828.[1] The lamps, chiefly of earthenware, form another class of objects on which such scenes are frequently portrayed, and to which broadly phallic forms are sometimes given. One of these phallic lamps is here represented, on the same plate with the bowl of Samian ware just described.[2] It is hardly necessary to explain the subject represented by this lamp, which was found in London a few years ago.

All this obscene pottery must be regarded, no doubt, as a proof of a great amount of dissoluteness in the morals of Roman society in Britain, but it is evidence of something more. It is hardly likely that such objects could be in common use at the family table; and we are led to suppose that they were employed on special occasions, festivals, perhaps, connected with the licentious worship of which we are

[1] Plate I, Fig. 1.
[2] Plate I, Fig. 2.

speaking, and such as those described in such strong terms in the satires of Juvenal. But monuments are found in this island which bear still more direct evidence to the existence of the worship of Priapus during the Roman period.

In the parish of Adel, in Yorkshire, are considerable traces of a Roman station, which appears to have been a place of some importance, and which certainly possessed temples. On the site of these were found altars, and other stones with inscriptions, which, after being long preserved in an outhouse of the rectory at Adel, are now deposited in the museum of the Philosophical Society at Leeds. One of the most curious of these, which we have here engraved for the first time,[1] apears to be a votive offering to Priapus, who seems to be addressed under the name of Mentula. It is a rough, unsquared stone, which has been selected for possessing a tolerably flat and smooth surface; and the figure and letters were made with a rude implement, and by an unskilled workman, who was evidently unable to cut a continuous smooth line. The middle of the stone is occupied by the figure of a phallus, and round it we read very distinctly the words:—

PRIMINVS MENTLA.

[1] Plate IV, Fig. 1.

The author of the inscription may have been an ignorant Latinist as well as unskilful sculptor, and perhaps mistook the ligulated letters, overlooking the limb which would make the L stand for VL, and giving A for AE. It would then read *Priminus Mentulæ*, Priminus to Mentula (the object personified), and it may have been a votive offering from some individual named Priminus, who was in want of an heir, or laboured under some sexual infirmity, to Priapus, whose assistance he sought. Another interpretation has been suggested, on the supposition that Mentla, or perhaps (the L being designed for IL ligulated) Mentila or Mentilla, might be the name of a female joined with her husband in this offering for their common good. The former of these interpretations seems, however, to be the most probable. This monument belongs probably to rather a late date in the Roman period. Another *ex voto* of the same class was found at Westerwood Fort in Scotland, one of the Roman fortresses on the wall of Antoninus. This monument [1] consisted of a square slab of stone, in the middle of which was a phallus, and under it the words EX : VOTO. Above were the let-

---

[1] See Plate IV, Fig. 2. Horseley, who engraved this monument in his *Brittania Romana*, Scotland, fig. xix. has inserted a fig-leaf in place of the phallus, but with slight indications of the form of the object it was intended to conceal. We are not aware if this monument is still in existence.

22

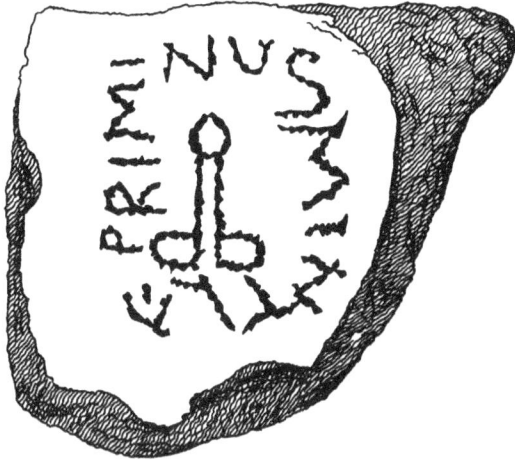

Fig 1.

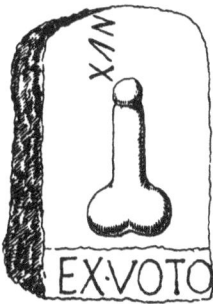

Fig 2

Fig 3

PLATE IV

PHALLIC MONUMENTS FOUND IN SCOTLAND

ters XAN, meaning, perhaps, that the offerer had laboured *ten years* under the grievance of which he sought redress from Priapus. We may point also to a phallic monument of another kind, which reminds us in some degree of the finer sculptures at Nîmes. At Housesteads, in Northumberland, are seen the extensive and imposing remains of one of the Roman stations on the Wall of Hadrian named Borcovicus. The walls of the entrance gateways are especially well preserved, and on that of the guard-house attached to one of them, is a slab of stone presenting the figure given in our plate IV, fig. 3. It is a rude delineation of a phallus with the legs of a fowl, and reminds us of some of the monuments in France and Italy previously described. These phallic images were no doubt exposed in such situations because they were supposed to exercise a protective influence over the locality, or over the building, and the individual who looked upon the figure believed himself safe, during that day at least, from evil influences of various descriptions. They are found, we believe, in some other Roman stations, in a similar position to that of the phallus at Housesteads.

Although the worship of which we are treating prevailed so extensively among the Romans and throughout the Roman provinces, it was far from being peculiar to them, for the same superstition formed part of the religion of the Teutonic race, and was carried with that race wherever it settled. The Teutonic god, who answered to the Roman Priapus, was called, in Anglo-Saxon, Fréa, in Old Norse, Freyr, and, in Old German, Fro. Among the Swedes, the principal seat of his worship was at Upsala, and Adam of Bremen, who lived in the eleventh century, when paganism still retained its hold on the north, in describing the forms under which the gods were there represented, tells us that " the third of the gods at Upsala was Fricco [another form of the name], who bestowed on mortals peace and pleasure, and who was represented *with an immense priapus;* " and he adds that, at the celebration of marriages, they offered sacrifice to Fricco. This god, indeed, like the Priapus of the Romans, presided over generation and fertility, either of animal life or of the produce of the earth, and was invoked accordingly. Ihre, in his *Glossarium Sueco-Gothicum,* mentions objects of antiquity dug up in the north of Europe, which clearly prove the prevalence of phallic rites. To this deity, or to his female representative of the same name, the Teutonic Venus, Friga, the fifth day of the week was dedicated, and on that account received its name, in Anglo-Saxon, Frige-dæg, and in modern English, Friday. Frigedæg appears to have been a name sometimes given in Anglo-Saxon to Frea himself; in a charter of the date of 959, printed in Kemble's *Codex Diplomaticus,* one of the marks on a boundary-line of land is Frigedæges-Tréow, meaning apparently Frea's tree, which was probably a tree dedicated to that god, and the scene of Priapic rites. There is a place called Fridaythorpe in Yorkshire, and Friston, a name which occurs in several parts of England, means, probably, the stone of Frea or of Friga; and we seem justified in supposing that this and other names commencing with the syllable Fri or Fry, are so many monuments of the existence of the phallic worship among our Anglo-Saxon forefathers. Two customs cherished among our old English popular superstitions are believed to have been derived from this worship, the need-fires, and the procession of the boar's head at the Christmas festivities. The former were fires kindled at the period of the summer solstice, and were certainly in their origin religious observances. The boar was intimately connected with the worship of Frea.[1]

From our want of a more intimate knowledge of this part of Teutonic paganism, we are unable to decide whether some of the superstitious practices of the middle ages were derived from the Romans or from the peoples who established themselves in the

---

[1] See Grimm's Deutsche Mythologie, p. 139, first edition.

---

provinces after the overthrow of the western empire; but in Italy and in Gaul (the southern parts especially), where the Roman institutions and sentiments continued with more persistence to hold their influence, it was the phallic worship of the Romans which, gradually modified in its forms, was thus preserved, and, though the records of such a worship are naturally accidental and imperfect, yet we can distinctly trace its existence to a very late period. Thus, we have clear evidence that the phallus, in its simple form, was worshipped by the mediæval Christians, and that the forms of Christian prayer and invocation were actually addressed to it. One name of the male organ among the Romans was *fascinum;* it was under this name that it was suspended round the necks of women and children, and under this name especially it was supposed to possess magical influences which not only acted upon others, but defended those who were under its protection from magical or other evil influences from without. Hence are derived the words to *fascinate* and *fascination.* The word is used by Horace, and especially in the epigrams of the *Priapeia,* which may be considered in some degree as the exponents of the popular creed in these matters. Thus we have in one of these epigrams the lines,—

"Placet, Priape ? qui sub arboris coma
Soles, sacrum revincte pampino caput,
Ruber sedere cum rebente *fascino*."
                                 Priap. Carm. lxxxiv.

It seems probable that this had become the popular, or vulgar, word for the phallus, at least taken in this point of view, at the close of the Roman power, for the first very distinct traces of its worship which we find afterwards introduce it under this name, which subsequently took in French the form *fesne*. The mediæval worship of the *fascinum* is first spoken of in the eighth century. An ecclesiastical tract entitled *Judicia Sacerdotalia de Criminibus*, which is ascribed to the end of that century, directs that " if any one has performed incantation to the *fascinum*, or any incantation whatever, except any one who chaunts the Creed or the Lord's Prayer, let him do penance on bread and water during three lents." An act of the council of Châlons, held in the ninth century, prohibits the same practice almost in the same words; and Burchardus repeats it again in the twelfth century,[1] a proof of the continued existence of this worship. That it was in full force long after this is proved by the statutes of the synod of Mans, held in 1247, which enjoin similarly the punishment for him " who has sinned to the fascinum, or has performed

---

[1] D. Burchardi *Decretorum libri*, lib. x, c 49.

any incantations, except the creed, the pater noster, or other canonical prayer." This same provision was adopted and renewed in the statutes of the synod of Tours, held in 1396, in which, as they were published in French, the Latin *fascinum* is represented by the French *fesne*. The *fascinum* to which such worship was directed must have been something more than a small amulet.

This brings us to the close of the fourteenth century, and shows us how long the outward worship of the generative powers, represented by their organs, continued to exist in Western Europe to such a point as to engage the attention of ecclesiastical synods. During the previous century facts occurred in our own island illustrating still more curiously the continuous existence of the worship of Priapus, and that under circumstances which remind us altogether of the details of the phallic worship under the Romans. It will be remembered that one great object of this worship was to obtain fertility either in animals or in the ground, for Priapus was the god of the horticulturist and the agriculturist. St. Augustine, declaiming against the open obscenities of the Roman festival of the Liberalia, informs us that an enormous phallus was carried in a magnificent chariot into the middle of the public place of the town with great ceremony, where the most respectable matron ad-

vanced and placed a garland of flowers " on this
obscene figure; " and this, he says,' was done to ap-
pease the god, and " to obtain an abundant harvest,
and remove enchantments from the land."[1] We learn
from the Chronicle of Lanercost that, in the year 1268,
a pestilence prevailed in the Scottish district of
Lothian, which was very fatal to the cattle, to coun-
teract which some of the clergy—*bestiales, habitu
claustrales, non animo*—taught the peasantry to make
a fire by the rubbing together of wood (this was the
need-fire), and to raise up the image of Priapus, as
a means of saving their cattle. " When a lay member
of the Cistercian order at Fenton had done this before the door of the hall, and had sprinkled the cattle with a dog's testicles dipped in holy water, and
complaint had been made of this crime of idolatry
against the lord of the manor, the latter pleaded in
his defence that all this was done without his knowledge and in his absence, but added, ' while until the
present month of June other people's cattle fell ill
and died, mine were always found, but now every
day two or three of mine die, so that I have few left
for the labours of the field.' " Fourteen years after
this, in 1282, an event of the same kind occurred at
Inverkeithing, in the present county of Fife in Scot-

[1] S. Augustini *De Civit. Dei*, lib. vii, c. 21.

land. The cause of the following proceedings is not stated, but it was probably the same as that for which the cistercian of Lothian had recourse to the worship of Priapus. In the Easter week of the year just stated (March 29—April 5), a parish priest of Inverkeithing, named John, performed the rites of Priapus, by collecting the young girls of the town, and making them dance round the figure of this god; without any regard for the sex of these worshippers, he carried a wooden image of the male members of generation before them in the dance, and himself dancing with them, he accompanied their songs with movements in accordance, and urged them to licentious actions by his no less licentious language. The more modest part of those who were present felt scandalized with the priest, but he treated their words with contempt, and only gave utterance to coarser obscenities. He was cited before his bishop, defended himself upon the common usage of the country, and was allowed to retain his benefice; but he must have been rather a worldly priest, after the style of the middle ages, for a year afterwards he was killed in a vulgar brawl.

The practice of placing the figure of a phallus on the walls of buildings, derived, as we have seen, from the Romans, prevailed also in the middle ages, and the buildings especially placed under the influence of this symbol were churches. It was believed to be

Fig 1.

Fig 3.

Fig 2

Fig 4.

PLATE V

SHELAH-NA-GIG MONUMENTS

a protection against enchantments of all kinds, of which the people of those times lived in constant terror, and this protection extended over the place and over those who frequented it, provided they cast a confiding look upon the image. Such images were seen, usually upon the portals, on the cathedral church of Toulouse, on more than one church in Bourdeaux, and on various other churches in France, but, at the time of the revolution, they were often destroyed as marks only of the depravity of the clergy. Dulaure tells us that an artist, whom he knew, but whose name he has not given, had made drawings of a number of these figures which he had met with in such situations. A Christian saint exercised some of the qualities thus deputed to Priapus; the image of St. Nicholas was usually painted in a conspicuous position in the church, for it was believed that whoever had looked upon it was protected against enchantments, and especially against that great object of popular terror, the evil eye, during the rest of the day.

It is a singular fact that in Ireland it was the female organ which was shown in this position of protector upon the churches, and the elaborate though rude manner in which these figures were sculptured, show that they were considered as objects of great importance. They represented a female exposing herself to view in the most unequivocal manner, and are carved on a block which appears to have served as the key-stone to the arch of the door-way of the church, where they were presented to the gaze of all who entered. They appear to have been found principally in the very old churches, and have been mostly taken down, so that they are only found among the ruins. People have given them the name of *Shelah-na-Gig,* which, we are told, means in Irish Julian the Giddy, and is simply a term for an immodest woman; but it is well understood that they were intended as protecting charms against the fascination of the evil eye. We have given copies of all the examples yet known in our plates v and vi. The first of these [1] was found in an old church at Rochestown, in the county of Tipperary, where it had long been known among the people of the neighbourhood by the name given above. It was placed in the arch over the doorway, but has since been taken away. Our second example of the Shelah-na-Gig [2] was taken from an old church lately pulled down in the county Cavan, and is now preserved in the museum of the Society of Antiquaries of Dublin. The third [3] was found at Ballinahend Castle, also in

[1] Plate v, Fig. 1.
[2] Plate v, Fig. 2.
[3] Plate v, Fig. 3.

the county of Tipperary; and the fourth [1] is preserved in the museum at Dublin, but we are not informed from whence it was obtained. The next,[2] which is also now preserved in the Dublin Museum, was taken from the old church on the White Island, in Lough Erne, county Fermanagh. This church is supposed by the Irish antiquaries to be a structure of very great antiquity, for some of them would carry its date as far back as the seventh century, but this is probably an exaggeration. The one which follows [3] was furnished by an old church pulled down by order of the ecclesiastical commissioners, and it was presented to the museum at Dublin, by the late Dean Dawson. Our last example [4] was formerly in the possession of Sir Benjamin Chapman, Bart., of Killoa Castle, Westmeath, and is now in a private collection in London. It was found in 1859 at Chloran, in a field on Sir Benjamin's estate known by the name of the " Old Town," from whence stones had been removed at previous periods, though there are now very small remains of building. This stone was found at a depth of about five feet from the surface, which shows that the building, a church no doubt,

---

[1] Plate v, Fig. 4.

[2] Plate vi, Fig. 1.

[3] Plate vi, Fig. 2.

[4] Plate vi, Fig. 3.

---

must have fallen into ruin a long time ago. Contiguous to this field, and at a distance of about two hundred yards from the spot where the Shelah-na-Gig was found, there is an abandoned churchyard, separated from the Old Town field only by a loose stone wall.

The belief in the salutary power of this image appears to be a superstition of great antiquity, and to exist still among all peoples who have not reached a certain degree of civilization. The universality of this superstition leads us to think that Herodotus may have erred in the explanation he has given of certain rather remarkable monuments of a remote antiquity. He tells us that Sesostris, king of Egypt, raised columns in some of the countries he conquered, on which he caused to be figured the female organ of generation as a mark of contempt for those who had submitted easily.[1] May not these columns have been intended, if we knew the truth, as protections for the people of the district in which they stood, and placed in the position where they could most conveniently been seen? This superstitious sentiment may also offer the true explanation of an incident which is

---

[1] Herodotus, Euterpe, cap. 102. Diodorus Siculus adds to the account given by Herodotus, that Sesostris also erected columns Learing the male generative organ as a compliment to the peoples who had defended themselves bravely.

Fig.1.

Fig 2.

Fig. 3.

PLATE VI

SHELAH-NA-GIG MONUMENTS

said to have been represented in the mysteries of Eleusis. Ceres, wandering over the earth in search of her daughter Proserpine, and overcome with grief for her loss, arrived at the hut of an Athenian peasant woman named Baubo, who received her hospitably, and offered her to drink the refreshing mixture which the Greeks call Cyceon (κυκεων). The goddess rejected the offered kindness, and refused all consolation. Baubo, in her distress, bethought her of another expedient to allay the grief of her guest. She relieved her sexual organs of that outward sign which is the evidence of puberty, and then presented them to the view of Ceres, who, at the sight, laughed, forgot her sorrows, and drank the cyceon.[1] The prevailing belief in the beneficial influence of this sight, rather than a mere pleasantry, seems to afford the best explanation of this story.

This superstition which, as shown by the Shelah-na-Gigs of the Irish churches, prevailed largely in the middle ages, explains another class of antiquities which are not uncommon. These are small figures of nude females exposing themselves in exactly the same

---

[1] This story is told by the two Christian Fathers, Arnobius, *Adversus Gentes*, lib. v. c. 5, and Clemens Alexandrinus *Protrepticus*, p. 17, ed. Oxon. 1715. The latter writer merely states that Baubo exposed her parts to the view of the goddess, without the incident of preparation mentioned by Arnobius.

manner as in the sculptures on the churches in Ireland just alluded to. Such figures are found not only among Roman, Greek, and Egyptian antiquities, but among every people who had any knowledge of art, from the aborigines of America to the far more civilized natives of Japan; and it would be easy to give examples from almost every country we know, but we confine ourselves to our more special part of the subject. In the last century, a number of small statuettes in metal, in a rude but very peculiar style of art, were found in the duchy of Mecklenburg-Strelitz, in a part of Germany formerly occupied by the Vandals, and by the tribe of the Obotrites, considered as a division of the Vendes. They appeared to be intended to represent some of the deities worshipped by the people who made them; and some of them bore inscriptions, one of which was in Runic characters. From this circumstance we should presume that they belonged to a period not much, if any, older than the fall of the Western Empire. Some time afterwards, a few statuettes in metal were found in the island of Sardinia, so exactly similar to those just mentioned, that D'Hancarville, who published an account of them with engravings, considered himself justified in ascribing them to the Vandals, who occupied that island, as well as the tract of Germany alluded to.[1] One of these images, which D'Hancarville considers to be the Venus of the Vandal mythology, represents a female in a reclining position, with the wings and claws of a bird, holding to view a pomegranate, open, which, as D'Hancarville remarks, was considered as a sign representing the female sexual organ. In fact, it was a form and idea more unequivocally represented in the Roman figures which we have already described,[2] but which continued through the middle ages, and was preserved in a popular name for that organ, *abricot,* or expressed more energetically, *abricot fendu,* used by Rabelais, and we believe still preserved in France. This curious image is represented, after D'Hancarville, in three different points of view in our plate.[3] Several figures of a similar description, but representing the subject in a more matter-of-fact shape, were brought from Egypt by a Frenchman who held an official situation in that country, and three of them are now in a private collection in London. We have engraved one of these small bronzes,[4] which, as will be seen, presents an exact counterpart of the Shelah-na-Gig.

[1] D'Hancarville, *Antiquities Etrusques, Grecques, et Romaines,* Paris, 1785, tom. v. p. 61.

[2] See our Plates ii, Fig. 4, vii, and Plate xii, Fig. 3.

[3] Plate vii, Figs. 1, 2, 3.

[4] Plate vii, Fig. 4.

These Egyptian images belonged no doubt to the Roman period. Another similar figure,[1] made of lead, and apparently mediæval, was found at Avignon, and is preserved in the same private collection just alluded to; and a third,[2] was dug up, about ten years ago, at Kingston-on-Thames. The form of these statuettes seems to show that they were intended as portable images, for the same purpose as the Shelahs, which people might have ready at hand to look upon for protection whenever they were under fear of the influence of the evil eye, or of any other sort of enchantment.

We have not as yet any clear evidence of the existence of the Shelah-na-Gig in churches out of Ireland. We have been informed that an example has been found in one of the little churches on the coast of Devon; and there are curious sculptures, which appear to be of the same character, among the architectural ornamentation of the very early church of San Fedele at Como in Italy. Three of these are engraved in our plate VIII. On the top of the right hand jamb of the door [3] is a naked male figure, and in the same position on the other side a female,[4]

1 Plate VII, Fig. 5.
2 Plate XII, Fig. 4.
3 Plate VIII, Fig. 1.
4 Plate VIII, Fig. 2.

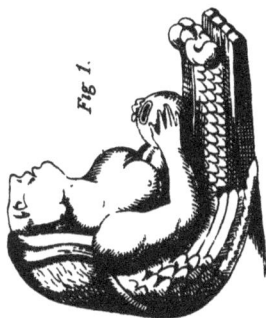

Fig. 3.

Fig. 6.

Fig. 2.

Fig 5

Fig. 1.

Fig. 4.

PLATE VII

VENUS OF THE VANDALS, BRONZE AND LEAD IMAGES, AND
CAPITAL OF A COLUMN

which are described to us as representing Adam and
Eve, and our informant, to whom we owe the drawings describes that at the apex [1] merely as "the
figure of a woman holding her legs apart." We understand that the surface of the stone in these sculptures is so much worn that it is quite uncertain
whether the sexual parts were ever distinctly marked,
but from the postures and positions of the hands, and
the situation in which these figures are placed, they
seem to resemble closely, except in their superior
style of art, the Shelah-na-Gigs of Ireland. There
can be little doubt that the superstition to which these
objects belonged gave rise to much of the indecent
sculpture which is so often found upon mediæval
ecclesiastical buildings. The late Baron von Hammer-
Pürgstall published a very learned paper upon monuments of various kinds which he considered as
illustrating the secret history of the order of the
Templars, from which we learn that there was in
his time a series of most extraordinary obscene sculptures in the church of Schoengraber in Austria, of
which he intended to give engravings, but the drawings had not arrived in time for his book; [2] but he
has engraved the capital of a column in the church of

[1] Plate VIII, Fig. 3.

[2] See Von Hammer-Pürgstall, *Fundgruben des Orients*, vol. vi,
p. 26.

Egra, a town of Bohemia, of which we give a copy,[1] in which the two sexes are displaying to view the members, which were believed to be so efficatious against the power of fascination.

The figure of the female organ, as well as the male, appears to have been employed during the middle ages of Western Europe far more generally than we might suppose, placed upon buildings as a talisman against evil influences, and especially against witchcraft and the evil eye, and it was used for this purpose in many other parts of the world. It was the universal practice among the Arabs of Northern Africa to stick up over the door of the house or tent, or put up nailed on a board in some other way, the generative organ of a cow, mare, or female camel, as a talisman to avert the influence of the evil eye. It is evident that the figure of this member was far more liable to degradation in form than that of the male, because it was much less easy, in the hands of rude draughtsmen, to delineate in an intelligible form, and hence it soon assumed shapes which though intended to represent it, we might rather call symbolical of it, though no symbolism was intended. Thus the figure of the female organ easily assumed the rude form of a horseshoe, and as the original

---

[1] Von Hammer-Pürgstall, *Fundgruben des Orients*, vol. vi, p. 35, and Plate iv, Fig. 31—See our Plate vii, Fig. 6.

meaning was forgotten, would be readily taken for that object, and a real horseshoe nailed up for the same purpose. In this way originated, apparently, from the popular worship of the generative powers, the vulgar practice of nailing a horseshoe upon buildings to protect them and all they contain against the power of witchcraft, a practice which continues to exist among the peasantry in some parts of England at the present day. Other marks are found, sometimes among the architectural ornaments, such as certain triangles and triple loops, which are perhaps typical forms of the same object. We have been informed that there is an old church in Ireland where the male organ is drawn on one side of the door, and the Shelah-na-Gig on the other, and that, though perhaps comparatively modern, their import as protective charms are well understood. We can easily imagine men, under the influence of these superstitions, when they were obliged to halt for a moment by the side of a building, drawing upon it such a figure, with the design that it should be a protection to themselves, and thus probably we derive from superstitious feelings the common propensity to draw phallic figures on the sides of vacant walls and in other places.

Antiquity had made Priapus a god, the middle ages raised him into a saint, and that under several names.

In the south of France, Provence, Languedoc, and the Lyonnais, he was worshipped under the title of St. Foutin.[1] This name is said to be a mere corruption of Fotinus or Photinus, the first bishop of Lyons, to whom, perhaps through giving a vulgar interpretation to the name, people had transferred the distinguishing attribute of Priapus. This was a large phallus of wood, which was an object of reverence to the women, especially to those who were barren, who scraped the wooden member, and, having steeped the scrapings in water, they drank the latter as a remedy against their barrenness, or administered it to their husbands in the belief that it would make them vigorous. The worship of this saint, as it was practiced in various places in France at the commencement of the seventeenth century, is described in that singular book, the *Confession de Sancy*.[2] We there learn that at Varailles in Provence, waxen images of the members of both sexes were offered to St. Foutin, and suspended to the ceiling of his chapel, and the writer remarks that, as the ceiling was covered with them, when the wind blew them about, it

---

[1] Our material for the account of these phallic saints is taken mostly from the work of M. Dulaure.

[2] La Confession de Sancy forms the fifth volume of the *Journal d'Henri III*, by Pierre de L'Estoile, ed. Duchat. See pp. 383, 391, of that volume.

produced an effect which was calculated to disturb very much the devotions of the worshippers. We hardly need remark that this is just the same kind of worship which existed at Isernia, in the kingdom of Naples, where it was presented in the same shape. At Embrun, in the department of the Upper Alps, the phallus of St. Foutin was worshipped in a different form; the women poured a libation of wine upon the head of the phallus, which was collected in a vessel, in which it was left till it became sour; it was then called the "sainte vinaigre," and the women employed it for a purpose which is only obscurely hinted at. When the Protestants took Embrun in 1585, they found this phallus laid up carefully among the relics in the principal church, its head red with the wine which had been poured upon it. A much larger phallus of wood, covered with leather, was an object of worship in the church of St. Eutropius at Orange, but it was seized by the Protestants and burnt publicly in 1562. St. Foutin was similarly an object of worship at Porigny, at Cives in the diocese of Viviers, at Vendre in the Bourbonnais, at Auxerre, at Puy-en-Velay, in the convent of Girouet near Sampigny, and in other places. At a distance of about four leagues from Clermont in Auvergne, there is (or was) an isolated rock, which presents the form of an immense phallus, and which is popularly called

51

St. Foutin. Similar phallic saints were worshipped under the names of St. Guerlichon, or Greluchon, at Bourg-Dieu in the diocese of Bourges, of St. Gilles in the Cotentin in Britany, of St. René in Anjou, of St. Regnaud in Burgundy, of St. Arnaud, and above all of St. Guignolé near Brest and at the village of La Chatelette in Berri. Many of these were still in existence and their worship in full practice in the last century; in some of them, the wooden phallus is described as being much worn down by the continual process of scraping, while in others the loss sustained by scraping was always restored by a miracle. This miracle, however, was a very clumsy one, for the phallus consisted of a long staff of wood passed through a hole in the middle of the body, and as the phallic end in front became shortened, a blow of a mallet from behind thrust it forward, so that it was restored to its original length.

It appears that it was also the practice to worship these saints in another manner, which also was derived from the forms of the worship of Priapus among the ancients, with whom it was the custom, in the nuptial ceremonies, for the bride to offer up her virginity to Priapus, and this was done by placing her sexual parts against the end of the phallus, and sometimes introducing the latter, and even completing the sacrifice. This ceremony is represented in a bas-relief in marble, an engraving of which is given in the *Musée Secret* of the antiquities of Herculaneum and Pompeii; its object was to conciliate the favour of the god, and to avert sterility. It is described by the early Christian writers, such as Lactantius and Arnobius, as a very common practice among the Romans; and it still prevails to a great extent over most part of the East, from India to Japan and the islands of the Pacific. In a public square in Batavia, there is a cannon taken from the natives and placed there as a trophy by the Dutch government. It presents the peculiarity that the touch-hole is made on a phallic hand, the thumb placed in the position which is called the "fig," and which we shall have to describe a little further on. It is always the same idea of reverence to the fertilizing powers of nature, of which the garland or the bunch of flowers was an appropriate emblem. There are traces of the existence of this practice in the middle ages. In the case of some of the priapic saints mentioned above, women sought a remedy for barrenness by kissing the end of the phallus; sometimes they appear to have placed a part of their body naked against the image of the saint, or to have sat upon it. This latter trait was perhaps too bold an adoption of the indecencies of pagan worship to last long, or to be praticed openly; but it appears to have been more innocently represented by lying upon the body of the saint, or sitting upon a stone, understood to represent him without the presence of the energetic member. In a corner in the church of the village of St. Fiacre, near Mouceaux in France, there is a stone called the chair of St. Fiacre, which confers fecundity upon women who sit upon it; but it is necessary that nothing should intervene between their bare skin and the stone. In the church of Orcival in Auvergne, there was a pillar which barren women kissed for the same purpose, and which had perhaps replaced some less equivocal object.[1] Traditions, at least, of similar practices were connected with St. Foutin, for it appears to have been the custom for girls on the point of marriage to offer their last maiden robe to that saint. This superstition prevailed to such an extent that it became proverbial. A story is told of a young bride who, on the wedding night, sought to deceive her husband on the question of her previous chastity, although, as the writer expresses it, " she had long ago deposited the robe of her virginity on the altar of St. Foutin." From this form of superstition is said to have arisen a vice which is understood to prevail especially in

---

[1] Dulaure relates that one day a villager's wife entering this church, and finding only a burly canon in it, asked him earnestly, " Where is the pillar which makes women fruitful ? " " I," said the canon, " I am the pillar."

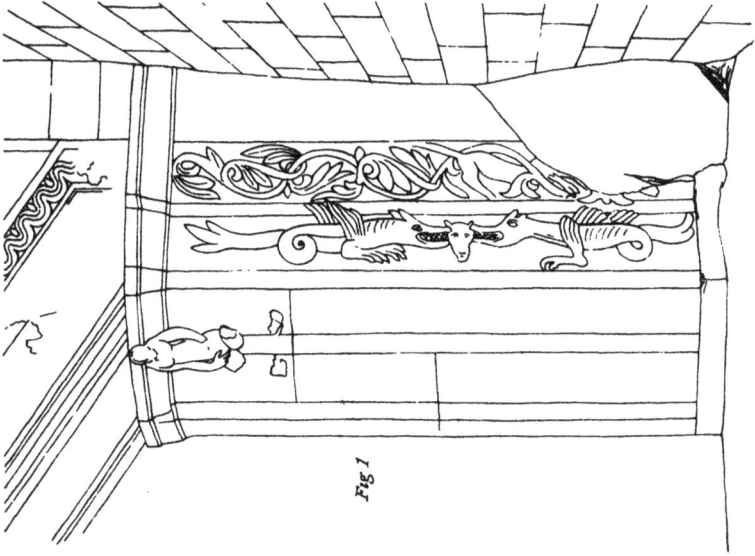

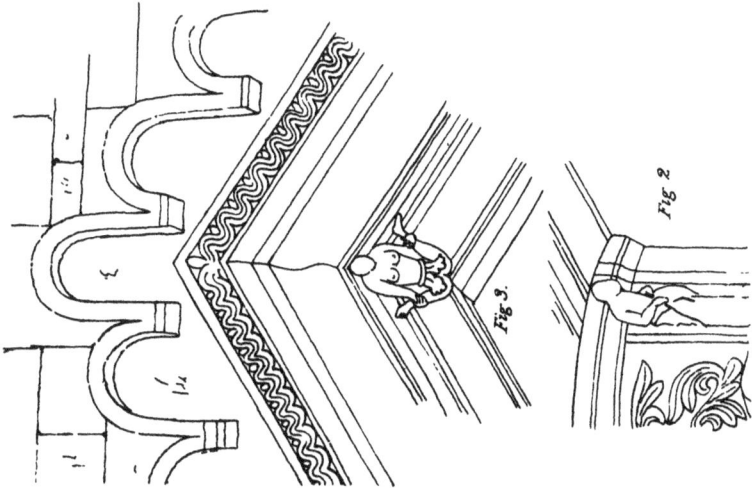

Fig 1

Fig 2

Fig 3

PLATE VIII

CAPITAL OF A COLUMN

nunneries—the use by women of artificial phalli, which appears in its origin to have been a religious ceremony. It certainly existed at a very remote period, for it is distinctly alluded to in the Scriptures,[1] where it is evidently considered as a part of pagan worship. It is found at an early period òf the middle ages, described in the Ecclesiastical Penitentials, with its appropriate amount of penitence. One of these penitential canons of the eighth century speaks of " a woman who, by herself or with the help of another woman, commits uncleanness," for which she was to do penance for three years, one on bread and water; and if this uncleanness was committed with a nun, the penance was increased to seven years, two only on bread and water. Another Penitential of an early date provides for the case in which both the women who participated in this act should be nuns; and Burchardus, bishop of Worms, one of the most celebrated authorities on such subjects, describes the instrument and use of it in greater detail. The practice had evidently lost its religious character and degenerated into a mere indulgence of the passions.

---

[1] Ezekiel, xvi, 17. Within a few years there has been a considerable manufacture of these objects in Paris, and it was understood that they were chiefly exported to Italy, where they were sold in the nunneries.

Antwerp has been described as the Lampsacus of Belgium, and Priapus was, down to a comparatively modern period, its patron saint, under the name of Ters, a word the deriviation of which appears to be unknown, but which was identical in meaning with the Greek *phallus* and the Latin *fascinum*. John Goropius Becan, who published a learned treatise on the antiquities of Antwerp in the middle of the sixteenth century, informs us how much this Ters was reverenced in his time by the Antwerpians, especially by the women, who invoked it on every occasion when they were taken by surprise or sudden fear.[1] He states that "if they let fall by accident a vessel of earthenware, or stumbled, or if any unexpected accident caused them vexation, even the most respectable women called aloud for the protection of Priapus under this obscene name." Goropius Becanus adds that there was in his time, over the door of a house adjoining the prison, a statue which had been furnished with a large phallus, then worn away or broken off. Among other writers who mention this statue is Abraham Golnitz, who published an account of his travels in France and Belgium, in 1631,[2] and he informs us that it was a carving in stone, about a foot

---

[1] Johannis Goropii Becani *Origines Antwerpianae*, 1569, lib. i, pp. 26, 101.

[2] Golnitzii *Itinerarium Belgico-Gallicum*, p. 52.

high, with its arms raised up, and its legs spread
out, and that the phallus had been entirely worn out
by the women, who had been in the habit of scraping
it and making a potion of the dust which they drank
as a preservative against barrenness. Golnitz further
tells us that a figure of Priapus was placed over the
entrance gate to the enclosure of the temple of St.
Walburgis at Antwerp, which some antiquaries
imagined to have been built on the site of a temple
dedicated to that deity. It appears from these writers
that, at certain times, the women of Antwerp deco-
rated the phalli of these figures with garlands.

The use of priapic figures as amulets, to be carried on the person as preservatives against the evil
eye and other noxious influences, which we have
spoken of as so common among the Romans, was
certainly continued through the middle ages, and, as
we shall see presently, has not entirely disappeared.
It was natural enough to believe that if this figure
were salutary when merely looked upon, it must be
much more so when carried constantly on the person. The Romans gave the name *fascinum*, in old
French *fesne*, to the phallic amulet, as well as to the
same figure under other circumstances. It is an object of which we could hardly expect to find direct
mention in mediæval writers, but we meet with examples of the object itself, usually made of lead (a

proof of its popular character), and ranging in date perhaps from the fourteenth to the earlier part of the sixteenth century. As we owe our knowledge of these phallic amulets almost entirely to one collector, M. Forgeais of Paris, who obtained them chiefly from one source—the river Seine, our present acquaintance with them may be considered as very limited, and we have every reason for believing that they had been in use during the earlier period. We can only illustrate this part of the subject by describing a few of these mediæval phallic amulets, which are preserved in some private collections; and we will first call attention to a series of objects, the real purpose of which appears to be very obscure. They are small leaden tokens or medalets, bearing on the obverse the figure of the male or female organ, and on the reverse a cross, a curious intimation of the adoption of the worship of the generative powers among Christians. These leaden tokens, found in the river Seine, were first collected and made known to antiquaries by M. Forgeais, who published examples of them in his work on the leaden figures found in that river.[1] We give five examples of the medals of each sex, obverse and reverse.[2] It will be seen that the phalli on

---

[1] Notice sur des Plombs Historiés trouvés dans la Seine, et recueillis par Arthur Forgeais. 8vo. Paris, 1858.

[2] See our Plate IX.

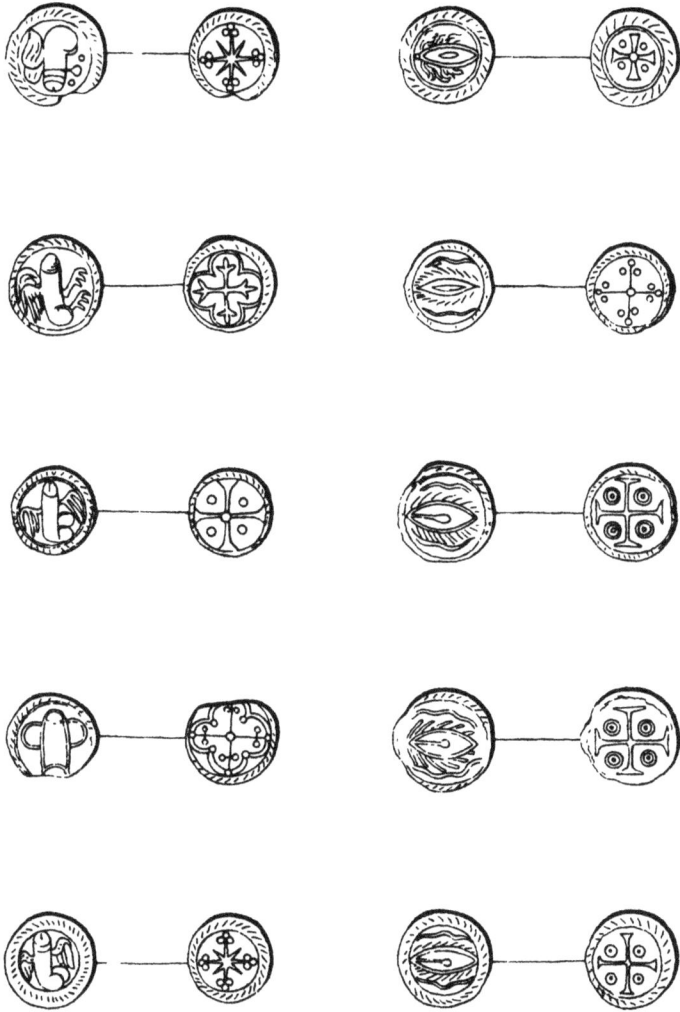

PLATE IX

ORNAMENTS FROM THE CHURCH OF SAN FEDELE

these tokens are nearly all furnished with wings; one has a bird's legs and claws; and on another there is an evident intention to represent a bell suspended to the neck . These characteristics show either a very distinct tradition of the forms of the Roman phallic ornament, or an imitation of examples of Roman phalli then existing—possibly the latter. But this is not necessary, for the bells borne by two examples, given in our next plate, and also taken from the collection of M. Forgeais are mediæval, and not Roman bells, though these also represent well-known ancient forms of treating the subject. In the first,[1] a female is riding upon the phallus, which has men's legs, and is held by a bridle. This figure was evidently intended to be attached to the dress as a brooch, for the pin which fixed it still remains on the back. Two other examples [2] present figures of winged phalli, one with a bell, and the other with the ring remaining from which the bell has no doubt been broken. One of these has the dog's legs. A fourth example [3] represents an enormous phallus attached to the middle of a small man. In another,[4] which was evidently intended for suspension, prob-

[1] Plate x, Fig. 1.
[2] Plate x, Figs. 2 and 3.
[3] Plate x, Fig. 4.
[4] Plate x, Fig. 5.

ably at the neck, the organs of the two sexes are joined together.   Three other leaden figures,[1] apparently amulets, which were in the Forgeais collection, offer a very peculiar variety of form, representing a figure, which we might suppose to be a male by its attributes, though it has a very feminine look, and wears the robe and hood of a woman. Its peculiarity consists in having a phallus before and behind. We have on the same plate [2] a still more remarkable example of the combination of the cross with the emblems of the worship of which we are treating, in an object found at San Agati di Goti, near Naples, which was formerly in the Beresford Fletcher collection, and is now in that of Ambrose Ruschenberger, Esq., of Boston, U. S. It is a *crux ansata*, formed by four phalli, with a circle of female organs round the centre; and appears by the loop to have been intended for suspension. As this cross is of gold, it had no doubt been made for some personage of rank, possibly an ecclesiastic; and we can hardly help suspecting that it had some connection with priapic ceremonies or festivities. The last figure on the same plate is also taken from the collection of M. Forgeais.[3] From the monkish cowl and the cord

---

[1] Plate xi, Figs. 1, 2, and 3.

[2] Plate xi, Fig. 4.

[3] Plate xi, Fig. 5.

---

round the body, we may perhaps take it for a satire upon the friars, some of whom wore no breeches, and they were all charged with being great corruptors of female morals.

In Italy we can trace the continuous use of these phallic amulets down to the present time much more distinctly than in our more Western countries. There they are still in very common use, and we give two examples [1] of bronze amulets of this description, which are commonly sold in Naples at the present day for a carlo, equivalent to fourpence in English money, each. One of them, it will be seen, is encircled by a serpent. So important are these amulets considered for the personal safety of those who possess them, that there is hardly a peasant who is without one, which he usually carries in his waistcoat pocket.

There was another, and less openly apparent, form of the phallus, which has lasted as an amulet during almost innumerable ages. The ancients had two forms of what antiquaries have named the phallic hand, one in which the middle finger was extended at length, and the thumb and other fingers doubled up, while in the other the whole hand was closed, but the thumb was passed between the first and middle

[1] Plate xii, Figs. 1 and 2.

fingers. The first of these forms appears to have
been the more ancient, and is understood to have
been intended to represent, by the extended middle
finger, the *membrum virile,* and by the bent fingers
on each side the testicles. Hence the middle finger
of the hand was called by the Romans, *digitus im-
pudicus,* or *infamis.* It was called by the Greeks
καταπύγων, which had somewhat the same meaning as
the Latin word, except that it had reference especially to degrading practices, which were then less
concealed than in modern times. To show the hand
in this form was expressed in Greek by the word
πκιμαλΐζειν, and was considered as a most contemptuous insult, because it was understood to intimate that
the person to whom it was addressed was addicted
to unnatural vice. This was the meaning also given to
it by the Romans, as we learn from the first lines of
an epigram of Martial:—

"Rideto, multum, qui te, Sextille, cinædum
Dixerit, et *digitum* porrigito *medium.*"

Martial, *Ep.* ii, 28.

Nevertheless, this gesture of the hand was looked
upon at an early period as an amulet against magical
influences, and, formed of different materials, it was
carried on the person in the same manner as the
phallus. It is not an uncommon object among Roman

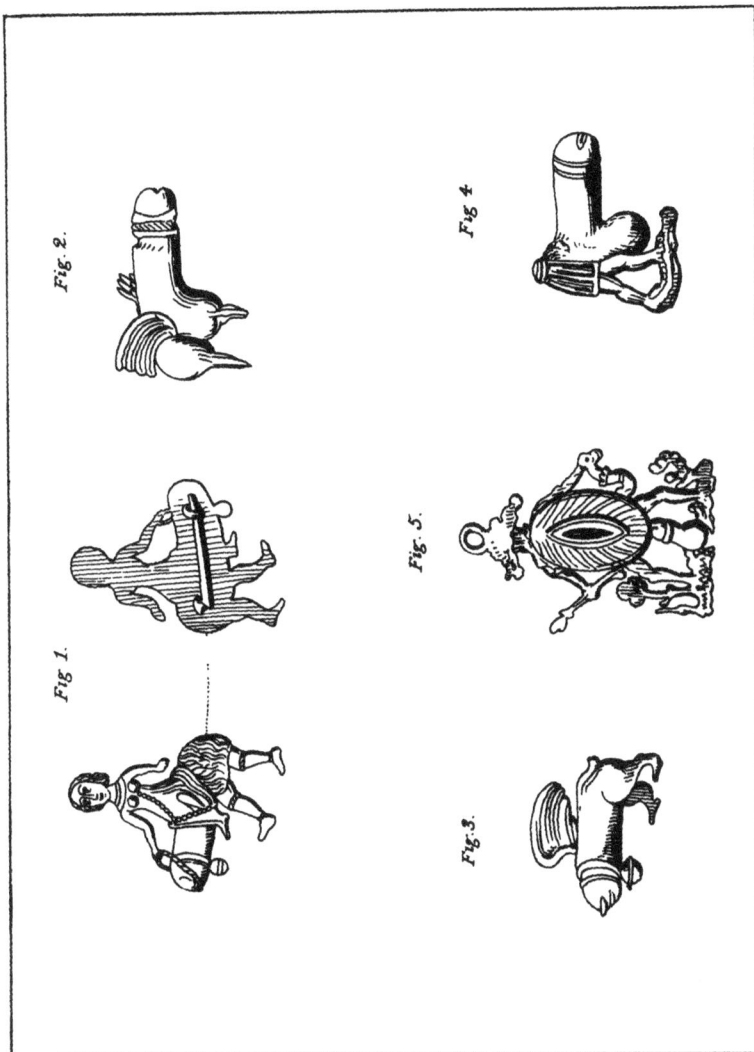

Fig. 2.

Fig 4

Fig 1.

Fig. 5.

Fig. 3.

PLATE X

PHALLIC LEADEN TOKENS FROM THE SEINE

antiquities, and was adopted by the Gnostics as one of their symbolical images. The second of these forms of the phallic hand, the intention of which is easily seen (the thumb forming the phallus), was also well known among the Romans, and is found made of various material, such as bronze, coral, lapis lazuli, and chrystal, of a size which was evidently intended to be suspended to the neck or to some other part of the person. In the *Musée Secret* at Naples, there are examples of such amulets, in the shape of two arms joined at the elbow, one terminating in the head of a phallus, the other having a hand arranged in the form just described, which seem to have been intended for pendents to ladies' ears. This gesture of the hand appears to have been called at a later period of Latin, though we have no knowledge of the date at which this use of the word began, *ficus*, a fig. *Ficus* being a word in the feminine gender, appears to have fallen in the popular language into the more common form of feminine nouns, *fica*, out of which arose the Italian *fica* (now replaced by *fico*), the Spanish *higa*, and the French *figue*. Florio, who gives the word *fica*, a fig, says that it was also used in the sense of " a woman's quaint," so that it may perhaps be classed with one or two other fruits, such as the pomegranate and the apricot, to which a similar erotic meaning was given.[1] The form, under this name, was preserved through the middle ages, especially in the South of Europe, where Roman traditions were strongest, both as an amulet and as an insulting gesture. The Italian called this gesture *fare la fica,* to make or do the fig to any one; the Spaniard, *dar una higa,* to give a fig; and the Frenchman, like the Italian, *faire la figue.* We can trace this phrase back to the thirteenth century at least. In the judicial proceedings against the Templars in Paris in 1309, one of the brethren of the Order was asked, jokingly, in his examination, because he was rather loose and flippant in his replies, " if he had been ordered by the said receptor (the officer of the Templars who admitted the new candidate) to make with his fingers the fig at the crucifix." Here the word used is the correct Latin *ficus;* and it is the same in the plural, in a document of the year 1449, in which an individual is said to have *made figs* with both hands at another. This phrase appears to have been introduced into the English language in the time of Elizabeth and to have been taken from the Spaniards, with whom our relations were then intimate. This we

---

[1] See before, page 43. Among the Romans, the fig was considered as a fruit consecrated to Priapus, on account, it is said, of its productiveness.

---

assume from the circumstance that the English phrase was " to give the fig " (*dar la higa*),[1] and that the writers of the Elizabethan age call it " the fig of Spain." Thus, " ancient " Pistol, in Shakespeare:—

> —— "A figo for thy friendship! —
> The fig of Spain." *Henry V*, iii. 6.

The phrase has been preserved in all these countries down to modern times and we still say in English, " a fig for anybody," or " for anything," not meaning that we estimate them at no more than the value of a fig, but that we throw at them that contempt which was intimated by showing them the phallic hand, and which the Greeks, as stated above, called σκιμαλίζειν. The form of showing contempt which was called the fig is still well known among the lower classes of society in England, and it is preserved in most of the countries of Western Europe. In Baretti's Spanish Dictionary, which belongs to the commencement of the present century, we find the word *higa* interpreted as "A manner of scoffing at people, which consists in showing the thumb between the first and second finger, closing the first, and pointing at the person to whom we want to give this hateful mark of contempt." Baretti also gives as still in use the original meaning of the word, "*Higa*, a little hand

---

[1] "Behold next I see contempt, *giving me the fico*." *Wit's Misery*, quoted in Nares, v. *Fico*.

made of jet, which they hang about children to keep
them from evil eyes; a superstitious custom." The
use of this amulet is still common in Italy, and especially in Naples and Sicily; it has an advantage
over the mere form of the phallus, that when the
artificial *fica* is not present, an individual, who finds
or believes himself in sudden danger, can make the
amulet with his own fingers. So profound is the
belief of its efficacy in Italy, that it is commonly
believed and reported there that, at the battle of
Solferino, the king of Italy held his hand in his
pocket with this arrangement of the fingers as a protection against the shots of the enemy.

There were personages connected with the worship
of Priapus who appear to have been common to the
Romans under and before the empire, and to the
foreign races who settled upon its ruins. The Teutonic race believed in a spiritual being who inhabited
the woods, and who was called in old German *scrat.*
His character was more general than that of a mere
habitant of the woods, for it answered to the English
hobgoblin, or to the Irish cluricaune. The scrat was
the spirit of the woods, under which character he
was sometimes called a *waltscrat,* and of the fields,
and also of the household, the domestic spirit, the
ghost haunting the house. His image was probably
looked upon as an amulet, a protection to the house,

Fig. 1

Fig. 2.

Fig. 3.

Fig. 4.

Fig 5.

PLATE XI

LEADEN ORNAMENTS FROM THE SEINE

as an old German vocabulary of the year 1482, explains *schrætlin*, little scrats, by the Latin word *penates*. The lascivious character of this spirit, if it wanted more direct evidence, is implied by the fact that *fcritta*, in Anglo-Saxon, and *scrat*, in old English, meant a hermaphrodite. Accordingly, the mediæval vocabularies explain *scrat* by Latin equivalents, which all indicate companions or emanations of Priapus, and in fact, Priapus himself. Isidore gives the name of *Pilosi*, or hairy men, and tells us that they were called in Greek, Panitæ (apparently an error for Ephialtæ), and in Latin, Incubi and Inibi, the latter word derived from the verb *inire*, and applied to them on account of their intercourse with animals. They were in fact the fauns and satyrs of antiquity, haunted like them the wild woods, and were characterized by the same petulance towards the other sex. Woe to the modesty of maiden or woman who ventured incautiously into their haunts. As Incubi, they visited the house by night, and violated the persons of the females, and some of the most celebrated heroes of early mediæval romances, such as Merlin, were thus the children of incubi. They were known at an early period in Gaul by the name of Dusii, from which, as the church taught that all these mythic personages were devils, we derive our modern word *Deuce*, used in such phrases as "the Deuce take you!" The term *ficarii* was also applied to them in mediæval Latin, either from the meaning of the word *ficus*, mentioned before,[1] or because they were fond of figs. Most of these Latin synonyms are given in the Anglo-Saxon vocabulary of Alfric, and are interpreted as meaning "evil men, spirits of the woods, evil beings." One of the old commentators on the Scriptures describes these spirits of the woods as "monsters in the semblance of men, whose form begins with the human shape and ends in the extremity of a beast." They were, in fact, half man, half goat, and were identical with a class of hobgoblins, who at a rather later period were well known in England by the popular name of Robin Goodfellows, whose Priapic character is sufficiently proved by the pictures of them attached to some of our early printed ballads, of which we give facsimiles. The first[2] is a figure of Robin Goodfellow, which forms the illustration to a very popular ballad of the earlier part of the seventeenth century, entitled "The mad merry Pranks of Robin Goodfellow;" he is represented party-coloured, and with the priapic attribute. The next[3] is a second il-

[1] See before, p. 70.

[2] See Plate XII, Fig. 5. From a copy of the black-letter ballad in the library of the British Museum.

[3] Plate XII, Fig. 2. From the same ballad.

lustration of the same ballad, in which Robin Good-fellow is represented as Priapus, goat-shaped, with his attributes still more strongly pronounced, and surrounded by a circle of his worshippers dancing about him. He appears here in the character assumed by the demon at the sabbath of the witches, of which we shall have to speak a little further on. The Romish Church created great confusion in all these popular superstitions by considering the mythic persons with whom they were connected as so many devils; and one of these Priapic demons is figured in a cut which seems to have been a favorite one, and is often repeated as an illustration of the broadside ballads of the age of James I. and Charles I.[1] It is Priapus reduced to his lowest step of degradation.

Besides the invocations addressed principally to Priapus, or to the generative powers, the ancients had established great festivals in their honour, which were remarkable for their licentious gaiety, and in which the image of the phallus was carried openly and in triumph. These festivities were especially celebrated among the rural population, and they were held chiefly during the summer months. The preparatory labours of the agriculturist were over,

---

[1] Plate xiii, Fig. 1. From two black-letter ballads in the British Museum, one entitled, " A warning for all Lewd Livers," the other, "A strange and true News from Westmoreland."

and people had leisure to welcome with joyfulness the activity of nature's reproductive powers, which was in due time to bring their fruits. Among the most celebrated of these festivals were the Liberalia, which were held on the 17th of March. A monstrous phallus was carried in procession in a car, and its worshippers indulged loudly and openly in obscene songs, conversation, and attitudes, and when it halted, the most respectable of the matrons ceremoniously crowned the head of the phallus with a garland. The Bacchanalia, representing the Dionysia of the Greeks, were celebrated in the latter part of October, when the harvest was completed, and were attended with much the same ceremonies as the Liberalia. The phallus was similarly carried in procesion, and crowned, and, as in the Liberalia, the festivities being carried on into the night, as the celebrators became heated with wine, they degenerated into the extreme of licentiousness, in which people indulged without a blush in the most infamous vices. The festival of Venus was celebrated towards the beginning of April, and in it the phallus was again carried in its car, and led in procession by the Roman ladies to the temple of Venus outside the Colline gate, and there presented by them to the sexual parts of the goddess. This part of the scene is represented in a well-known intaglio, which has

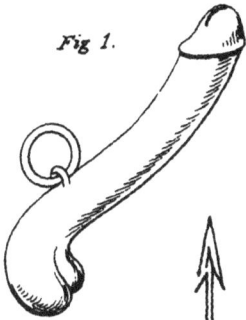

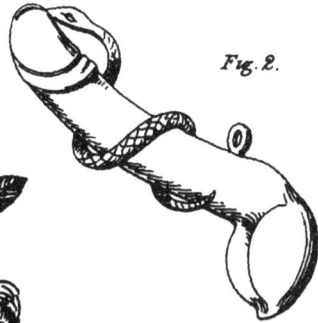

Fig 1.

Fig. 2.

Fig. 4

Fig 5.

Fig 3.

PLATE XII

AMULETS OF GOLD AND LEAD

been published in several works on antiquities. At the close of the month last mentioned came the Floralia, which, if possible, excelled all the others in licence. Ausonius, in whose time (the latter half of the fourth century) the Floralia were still in full force, speaks of their lasciviousness—

> Nec non lascivi Floralia læta theatri,
> Quæ spectare volunt qui voluisse negant.
> Ausonii *Eclog. de Feriis Romanis.*

The loose women of the town and its neighbourhood, called together by the sounding of horns, mixed with the multitude in perfect nakedness, and excited their passions with obscene motions and language, until the festival ended in a scene of mad revelry, in which all restraint was laid aside. Juvenal describes a Roman dame of very depraved manners as—

> . . . . Dignissima prorsus
> Florali matrona tuba.
> Juvenalis *Sat.* vi, 1. 249.

These scenes of unbounded licence and depravity, deeply rooted in people's minds by long established customs, caused so little public scandal, that it is related of Cato the younger that, when he was present at the celebration of the Floralia, instead of showing any disapproval of them, he retired, that his well-known gravity might be no restraint upon them, because the multitude manifested some hesitation in stripping the women naked in the presence of a man so celebrated for his modesty. The festivals more specially dedicated to Priapus, the Priapeia, were attended with similar ceremonies and similarly licentious orgies. Their forms and characteristics are better known, because they are so frequently represented to us as the subjects of works of Roman art. The Romans had other festivals of similar character, but of less importance, some of which were of a more private character, and some were celebrated in strict privacy. Such were the rites of the Bona Dea, established among the Roman matrons in the time of the republic, the disorders of which are described in such glowing language by the satirist Juvenal, in his enumeration of the vices of the Roman women:—

Nota Bonæ secreta Deæ, quum tibia lumbos
Incitat, et cornu pariter vinoque feruntur
Attonitæ, crinemque rotant, ululantque Priapi
Mænades. O quantus tunc illis mentibus ardor
Concubitus! quæ vox saltante libidine! quantus
Ille meri veteris per crura madentia torrens!
Lenonum ancillas posita Saufeia corona
Provocat, et tollit pendentis præmia coxæ.
Ipsa Medullinæ fluctum crissantis adorat.
Palmam inter dominas virtus natalibus æquat.
Nil ibi per ludum simulabitur: omnia fient
Ad verum, quibus incendi jam frigidus ævo
Laomedontiades et Nestoris hernia possit.
Tunc prurigo moræ impatiens, tunc femina simplex,
Et toto pariter repetitus clamor ab antro:
Jam fas est: admitte viros! —Juvenalis *Sat.* vi, l. 314.

Among the Teutonic, as well as among most other peoples, similar festivals appear to have been celebrated during the summer months; and, as they arose out of the same feelings, they no doubt presented the same general forms. The principal popular festivals of the summer during the middle ages occurred in the months of April, May, and June, and comprised Easter, May-day, and the feast of the summer solstice. All these appear to have been originally accompanied with the same phallic worship which formed the principal characteristic of the great Roman festivals; and, in fact, these are exactly those popular institutions and traits of popular manners which were most likely to outlive, also without any material change, the overthrow of the Roman empire by the barbarians. Although, at the time when we become intimately acquainted with these festivals, most of the prominent marks of their phallic character had been abandoned and forgotten, yet we meet during the interval with scattered indications which leave no room to doubt of their former existence. It will be interesting to examine into some of these points, and to show the influence they exerted on mediæval society.

The first of the three great festivals just mentioned was purely Anglo-Saxon and Teutonic; but it appears in the first place to have been identified with the

Roman Liberalia, and it was further transformed by
the Catholic church into one of the great Christian
religious feasts. In the primitive Teutonic mythology
there was a female deity named, in Old German,
Ostara, and, in Anglo-Saxon, *Eastre,* or *Eostre,* but
all we know of her is the simple statement of our
father of history, Bede, that her festival was celebrated by the ancient Saxons in the month of April,
from which circumstance, that month was named by
the Anglo-Saxons *Easter-monath,* or *Eoster-monath,*
and that the name of the goddess had been subsequently given to the Paschal time, with which it was
identical. The name of this goddess was given to
the same month by the old Germans and by the
Franks, so that she must have been one of the most
highly honoured of the Teutonic deities, and her
festival must have been a very important one, and
deeply implanted in the popular feelings, or the
church would not have sought to identify it with one
of the greatest Christian festivals of the year. It is
understood that the Romans considered this month
as dedicated to Venus, no doubt because it was that
in which the productive power of nature began to be
visibly developed. When the Pagan festival was
adopted by the church, it became a moveable feast
instead of being fixed to the month of April. Among
other objects offered to the goddess at this time were

84

Fig. 1.

Fig. 2.

PLATE XIII
ROBIN GOODFELLOW AND PHALLIC ORNAMENTS

cakes, made no doubt of fine flour, but of their form we are ignorant. The Christians, when they seized upon the Easter festival, gave them the form of a bun, which, indeed, was at that time the ordinary form of bread; and to protect themselves, and those who eat them, from any enchantment, or other evil influences which might arise from their former heathen character, they marked them with the Christian symbol—the cross. Hence were derived the cakes we still eat at Easter under the name of hot-cross-buns, and the superstitious feelings attached to them, for multitudes of people still believe that if they failed to eat a hot-cross-bun on Good-Friday they would be unlucky all the rest of the year. But there is some reason for believing that, at least in some parts, the Easter-cakes had originally a different form—that of the phallus. Such at least appears to have been the case in France, where the custom still exists. In Saintonge, in the neighbourhood of La Rochelle, small cakes, baked in the form of a phallus, are made as offerings at Easter, and are carried and presented from house to house; and we have been informed that similar practices exist in some other places. When Dulaure wrote, the festival of Palm Sunday, in the town of Saintes, was called the *fête des pinnes, pinne* being a popular and vulgar word for the *membrum virile.* At this *fête* the women

and children carried in the procession, at the end of
their palm branches, a phallus made of bread, which
they called undisguisedly a *pinne,* and which, having
been blest by the priest, the women carefully preserved during the following year as an amulet. A
similar practice existed at St. Jean-d'Angély, where
small cakes, made in the form of the phallus, and
named *fateux,* were carried in the procession of the
Fête-Dieu, or Corpus Christi.[1] Shortly before the
time when Dulaure wrote, this practice was sup-
pressed by a new sous-préfet, M. Maillard. The custom of making cakes in the form of the sexual members, male and female, dates from a remote antiquity
and was common among the Romans. Martial made
a phallus of bread (*Priapus siligineus*) the subject of
an epigram of two lines:—

Si vis esse satur, nostrum potes esse priapum:
Ipse licet rodas inguina, purus eris.
Martial, lib. xiv, ep. 69.

The same writer speaks of the image of a female organ made of the same material in another of his
epigrams, to explain which, it is only necessary to
state that these images were composed of the finest
wheaten flour (*siligo*):—

---

[1] Dulaure, *Histoire Abrégée des Différent Cultes*, vol. ii, p. 285.
Second Edition. It was printed in 1825.

Pauper amicitiæ cum sis, Lupe, non es amicæ;
Et queritur de te mentula sola nihil.
Illa siligineis pinguescit adultera cunnis;
Convivam pascit nigra farina tuum.

Martial, lib. ix, ep. 3.

This custom appears to have been preserved from the Romans through the middle ages, and may be traced distinctly as far back as the fourteenth or fifteenth century. We are informed that in some of the earlier inedited French books on cookery, receipts are given for making cakes in these obscene forms, which are named without any concealment; and the writer on this subject, who wrote in the sixteenth century, Johannes Bruerinus Campegius, describing the different forms in which cakes were then made, enumerates those of the secret members of both sexes, a proof, he says of " the degeneracy of manners, when Christians themselves can delight in obscenities and immodest things even among their articles of food." He adds that some of these were commonly spoken of by a gross name, *des cons sucrés*. When Dulaure wrote, that is just forty years ago, cakes of these forms continued to be made in various parts of France, and he informs us that those representing the male organ were made in the Lower Limousin, and especially at Brives, while similar images of the female organ were made at Clermont in Auvergne, and in other places. They were popularly called *miches*.[1]

There is another custom attached to Easter, which has probably some relation to the worship of which we are treating, and which seems once to have prevailed throughout England, though we believe it is now confined to Shropshire and Cheshire. In the former county it is called *heaving*, in the latter *lifting*. On Easter Monday the men go about with chairs, seize the women they meet, and, placing them in the chairs, raise them up, turn them round two or three times, and then claim the right of kissing them. On Easter Tuesday, the same thing is done by the women to the men. This, of course, is only practiced now among the lower classes, except sometimes as a frolic among intimate friends. The chair appears to have been a comparatively modern addition, since such articles have become more abundant. In the last century four or five of the one sex took the victim of the other sex by the arms and legs, and lifted her or him in that manner, and the operation was attended, at all events on the part of the men, with much indecency. The women usually expect a small contribution of money from the men they have lifted. More anciently, in the time of Durandus, that is, in

[1] Dulaure, vol. ii, pp. 255-257.

the thirteenth century, a still more singular custom prevailed on these two days. He tells us that in many countries, on the Easter Monday, it was the rule for the wives to beat their husbands, and that on the Tuesday the husbands beat their wives. Brand, in his *Popular Antiquities,* tells us that in the city of Durham, in his time, it was the custom for the men, on the one day, to take off the women's shoes, which the latter were obliged to purchase back, and that on the other day the women did the same to the men.

In mediæval poetry and romance, the month of May was celebrated above all others as that consecrated to Love, which seemed to pervade all nature, and to invite mankind to partake in the general enjoyment. Hence, among nearly all peoples, its approach was celebrated with festivities, in which, under various forms, worship was paid to Nature's reproductiveness. The Romans welcomed the approach of May with their Floralia, a festival we have already described as remarkable for licentiousness; and there cannot be a doubt that our Teutonic forefathers had also their festival of the season long before they became acquainted with the Romans. Yet much of the mediæval celebration of May-day, especially in the South, appears to have been derived from the Floralia of the latter people. As in the Floralia, the arrival of the festival was announced by the sounding of horns during the preceding night, and no sooner had midnight arrived than the youth of both sexes proceeded in couples to the woods to gather branches and make garlands, with which they were to return just at sunrise for the purpose of decorating the doors of their houses. In England the grand feature of the day was the Maypole. This maypole was the stem of a tall young tree cut down for the occasion, painted of various colours, and carried in joyous procession, with minstrels playing before, until it reached the village green, or the open space in the middle of a town, where it was usually set up. It was there decked with garlands and flowers, the lads and girls danced round it, and people indulged in all sorts of riotous enjoyments. All this is well described by a Puritan writer of the reign of Queen Elizabeth—Philip Stubbes—who says that, " against Maie," " every parishe, towne, and village assemble themselves together, bothe men, women, and children, olde and yong, even all indifferently; and either goyng all together, or devidyng themselves into companies, they goe some to the woodes and groves, some to the hilles and mountaines, some to one place, some to another, where they spend all the night in pleasant pastymes, and in the mornyng thei returne, bryngyng with them birch bowes and braunches of trees to deck their assemblies withall, ... But their cheerest jewell thei bryng from thence is their Maie pole, whiche thei bryng home with greate veneration, as thus: Thei have twentie or fourtie yoke of oxen, every oxe havyng a sweete nosegaie of flowers placed on the tippe of his hornes, and these oxen drawe home this Maie poole (this stinckyng idoll rather), whiche is covered all over with flowers and hearbes, bound rounde about with strynges, from the top to the bottome, and sometyme painted with variable colours, with twoo or three hundred men, women, and children following it, with greate devotion. And thus beyng reared up, with handekerchiefes and flagges streamyng on the toppe, thei strawe the grounde aboute, binde greene boughes about it, sett up sommer haules, bowers, and arbours hard by it. And then fall thei to banquet and feast, to leape and daunce aboute it, as the heathen people did, at the dedication of their idolles, whereof this is a perfect patterne, or rather the thyng itself." [1]

The Puritans were deeply impressed with the belief that the maypole was a substantial relic of Paganism; and they were no doubt right. There appears to be reason sufficient for supposing that, at a period which cannot now be ascertained, the maypole had taken the place of the phallus. The ceremonies at-

[1] Stubbes, *Anatomie of Ahuses*, fol. 94, 8vo. London, 1583.

tending the elevation of the two objects were identical. The same joyous procession in the Roman festivals, described above, conducted the phallus into the midst of the town or village, where in the same manner it was decked with garlands, and the worship partook of the same character. We may add, too, that both festivals were attended with the same licentiousness. " I have heard it credibly reported," says the Puritan Stubbes, " and that *viva voce* by menne of greate gravitie and reputation, that of fourtie, three score, or a hundred maides goyng to the woode over night, there have scarcely the third part returned home again undefiled."

The day generally concluded with bonfires. These represented the need-fire, which was intimately connected with the ancient priapic rites. Fire itself was an object of worship, as the most powerful of the elements; but it was supposed to lose its purity and sacred character in being propagated from one material to another, and the worshippers sought on these solemn occasions to produce it in its primitive and purest form. This was done by the rapid friction of two pieces of wood, attended with superstitious ceremonies; the pure element of fire was believed to exist in the wood, and to be thus forced out of it, and hence it was called need-fire (in Old German *not-feur*, and in Anglo-Sayon, *neod-fyr*), meaning literally a forced fire, or fire extracted by force. Before the process of thus extracting the fire from the wood, it was necessary that all the fires previously existing in the village should be extinguished, and they were afterwards revived from the bonfire which had been lit from the need-fire. The whole system of bonfires originated from this superstition; they had been adopted generally on occasions of popular rejoicing, and the bonfires commemorating the celebrated gunpowder plot are only particular applications of the general practice to an accidental case. The superstition of the need-fire belongs to a very remote antiquity in the Teutonic race, and existed equally in ancient Greece. It is proscribed in the early capitularies of the Frankish emperors of the Carlovingian dynasty. The universality of this superstition is proved by the circumstance that it still exists in the Highlands of Scotland, especially in Caithness, where it is adopted as a protection for the cattle when attacked by disease which the Highlanders attribute to witchcraft.[1] It was from the remotest ages the custom to cause cattle, and even children, to pass across the need-fire, as a protection to them for the rest of their lives. The need-fire was kindled at Easter, on May-day, and especially at the

---

[1] Logan, *The Scottish Gael*, vol. ii, p. 64, and Jamieson's *Scottish Dictionary*, Suppl. sub. v. *Neidfyre*.

---

summer solstice, on the eve of the feast of St. John the Baptist, or of Midsummer-day.[1]

The eve of St. John was in popular superstition one of the most important days of the mediæval year. The need-fire—or the St. John's fire, as it was called—was kindled just at midnight, the moment when the solstice was supposed to take place, and the young people of both sexes danced round it, and, above all things, leaped over it, or rushed through it, which was looked upon not only as a purification, but as a protection against evil influences. It was the night when ghosts and other beings of the spiritual world were abroad, and when witches had most power. It was believed, even, that during this night people's souls left the body in sleep, and wandered over the world, separated from it. It was a night of the great meetings of the witches, and it was that in which they mixed their most deadly poisons, and performed their most effective charms. It was a night especially favourable to divination in every form, and in which maidens sought to know their future sweethearts and husbands. It was during this night, also, that plants possessed their greatest powers either for good or for evil, and that they were dug up with all due ceremonies and cautions. The more hidden virtues of

[1] See Grimm, *Deutsche Mythologie*, pp. 341-349.

plants, indeed, depended much on the time at which, and the ceremonies with which, they were gathered, and these latter were extremely superstitious, no doubt derived from the remote ages of paganism. As usual, the clergy applied a half-remedy to the evil; they forebade any rites or incantations in the gathering of medicinal herbs except by repeating the creed and the Lord's prayer.

As already stated, the night of St. John's, or Mid-summer-eve, was that when ghosts and spirits of all descriptions were abroad, and when witches assembled, and their potions, for good or for evil, and charms were made with most effect. It was the night for popular divination, especially among the young maidens, who sought to know who were destined to be their husbands, what would be their characters, and what their future conduct. The medicinal virtues of many plants gathered on St. John's eve, and with the due ceremonies, were far more powerful than if gathered at other times. The most secret practices of the old popular superstitions are now mostly forgotten, but when, here and there, we meet with a few traces of them, they are of a character which leads us to believe that they belonged to a great extent to that same worship of the generative powers which prevailed so generally among all peoples. We remember that, we believe in one of the earlier editions of Mother Bunch, maidens who wished to know if their lovers were constant or not were directed to go out exactly at midnight on St. John's eve, to strip themselves entirely naked, and in that condition to proceed to a plant or shrub, the name of which was given, and round it they were to form a circle and dance, repeating at the same time certain words which they had been taught by their instructress. Having completed this ceremony, they were to gather leaves of the plant round which they had danced, which they were to carry home and place under their pillows, and what they wished to know would be revealed to them in their dreams. We have seen in some of the mediæval treatises on the virtue of plants directions for gathering some plants of especial importance, in which it was required that this should be performed by young girls in a similar state of complete nakedness.

Plants and flowers were, indeed, intimately connected with this worship. We have seen how constantly they are introduced in the form of garlands, and they were always among the offerings to Priapus. It was the universal practice, in dancing round the fire on St. John's eve, to conclude by throwing various kinds of flowers and plants into it, which were considered to be propitiatory, to avert certain evils to which people were liable during the following year. Among the plants they offered are mentioned mother-wort, vervain, and violets. It is perhaps to this connection of plants with the old priapic worship that we owe the popular tendency to give them names which were more or less obscene, most of which are now lost, or are so far modified as to present no longer the same idea. Thus the well-known arum of our hedge-bottoms received the names, no doubt suggested by its form, of cuckoo's pintle, or priest's pintle, or dog's pintle; and, in French, those of *vit de chien* and *vit de prestre;* in English it is now abbreviated into cuckoo-pint, or, sometimes, cuckoo-point. The whole family of the orchides was distinguished by a corresponding word, accompanied with various qualifications. We have in William Coles's *Adam in Eden,* (fol. 1659) the different names, for different varieties, of doggs-stones, fool-stones, fox-stones; in the older *Herbal* of Gerard (fol. 1597) triple ballockes, sweet ballockes, sweet cods, goat's-stones, hare's-stones, &c.; in French, *couillon de bouc* (the goat was especially connected with the priapic mysteries) and *couille,* or *couillon de chien.* In French, too, as we learn from Cotgrave and the herbals, "a kind of sallet hearbe" was called *couille à l' évêque;* the greater stone-crop was named *couille au loup;* and the spindle-tree was known by the name of *couillon de prêtre.* There are several plants which possess somewhat the appearance of a rough bush of hair. One of these, a species of *adiantum*, was known even in Roman times by the name of *Capillus Veneris*, and in more modern times it has been called maiden-hair, and our lady's hair. Another plant, the *asplenium trichomanes*, was and is also called popularly maiden-hair, or maiden's-hair; and we believe that the same name has been given to one or two other plants. There is reason for believing that the hair implied in these names was that of the pubes.[1] We might collect a number of other old popular names of plants of a similar character with these just enumerated.

In an old calendar of the Romish church, which is often quoted in Brand's *Popular Antiquities*, the seeking of plants for their hidden virtues and magical properties is especially noted as part of the practices on the eve of St. John (*herbæ diversi generis quæruntur*); and one plant is especially specified in terms too mysterious to be easily understood. Fern-seed, also, was a great object of search on this night; for, if found and properly gathered, it was believed to possess powerful magical properties, and especially

[1] Fumitory was another of these plants, and in a vocabulary of plants in a MS. of the middle of the thirteenth century, we find its names in Latin, French, and English given as follows, "*Fumus terrae, fumeterre, cunteboare.*" See Wright's *Volume of Vocabularies*, p. 17.

that of rendering invisible the individual who carried it upon his person. But the most remarkable of all the plants connected with these ancient priapic superstitions was the mandrake (*mandragora*), a plant which has been looked upon with a sort of feeling of reverential fear at all periods, and almost in all parts. Its Teutonic name, *alrun*, or, in its more modern form, *alraun*, speaks at once of the belief in its magical qualities among that race. People looked upon it as possessing some degree of animal life, and it was generally believed that, when it was drawn out of the earth, it uttered a cry, and that this cry carried certain death or madness to the person who extracted it. To escape this danger, the remedy was to tie a string round it, which was to be attached to a dog, and the latter, being driven away, dragged up the root in its attempt to run off, and experienced the fatal consequences. The root was the important part of the plant; it has somewhat the form of a forked radish, and was believed to represent exactly the human form below the waist, with, in the male and female plants, the human organs of generation distinctly developed. The mandrake, when it could be obtained, was used in the middle ages in the place of the phallic amulet, and was carefully carried on the person, or preserved in the house. It conferred fertility in more senses than one, for it was believed that as long as you kept it locked up with your money, the latter would become doubled in quantity every year; and it had at the same time all the protective qualities of the phallus. The Templars were accused of worshipping the mandrake, or *mandragora,* which became an object of great celebrity in France during the reigns of the weak monarchs Charles VI. and Charles VII. In 1429 one Friar Richard, of the order of the Cordeliers, preached a fierce sermon against the use of this amulet, the temporary effect of which was so great, that a certain number of his congregation delivered up their "mandragoires" to the preacher to be burnt.[1]

It appears that the people who dealt in these amulets helped nature to a rather considerable extent by the means of art, and that there was a regular process of cooking them up. They were necessarily aware that the roots themselves, in their natural state, presented, to say the least, very imperfectly the form which men's imagination had given to them, so they obtained the finest roots they could, which, when fresh from the ground, were plump and soft, and readily took any impression which might be given to them. They then stuck grains of millet or barley into the parts where they wished to have hair, and again

---

[1] *Journal a'un Bourgeois de Paris,* under the year 1429.

---

put it into a hole in the earth, until these grains had germinated and formed their roots. This process, it was said, was perfected within twenty days. They then took up the mandrake again, trimmed the fibrous roots of millet or barley which served for hair, retouched the parts themselves so as to give them their form more perfectly and more permanently, and then sold it.[1]

Besides these great and general priapic festivals, there were doubtless others of less importance, or more local in their character, which degenerated in aftertimes into mere local ceremonies and festivities. This would be the case especially in cities and corporate towns, where the guilds came in, to perpetuate the institution, and to give it gradually a modified form. Most towns in England had once festivals of this character, and at least three representatives of them are still kept up, the procession of Lady Godiva at Coventry, the Shrewsbury show, and the guild festival at Preston in Lancashire. In the first of these, the lady who is supposed to ride naked in the procession probably represents some feature in the ancient priapic celebration; and the story of the manner in which the Lady Godiva averted the anger of her husband from the townsmen, which is certainly a mere

[1] See the authorities for these statements in Dulaure, pp. 254—256.

fable, was no doubt invented to explain a feature of the celebration, the real meaning of which had in course of time been forgotten. The pageantry of the Shrewsbury show appears to be similarly the unmeaning reflection of forms belonging to older and forgotten practices and principles. On the Continent there were many such local festivals, such as the feast of fools, the feast of asses (the ass was an animal sacred to Priapus), and others, all which were adapted by the mediæval church exactly as the clergy had taken advantage of the profit to be derived from the phallic worship in other forms.

The leaden tokens, or medalets, which we have already described,[1] seem to point evidently to the existence in the middle ages of secret societies or clubs connected with this obscene worship, besides the public festivals. Of these it can hardly be expected that any description would survive, but, if not the fact, the belief in it is clearly established by the eagerness with which such obscene rites were laid to the charge of most of the mediæval secret societies, whether lay clubs or religious sects, and we know that secret societies abounded in the middle ages. However willing the Romish clergy were to make profit out of the popular phallic worship, they were

[1] See before, p. 60, and Plate IX.

equally ready to use the belief in it as a means of exciting prejudice against any sects which the church chose to regard as religious or political heretics.

It is very evident that, in the earlier ages of the church, the conversion of the Pagans to Christianity was in a vast number of cases less than a half-conversion, and that the preachers of the gospel were satisfied by people assuming the name of Christians, without inquiring too closely into the sincerity of their change, or into their practice. We can trace in the expressions of disapproval in the writings of some of the more zealous of the ecclesiastical writers, and in the canons of the earlier councils, the alarm created by the prevalence among Christians of the old popular festivals of paganism; and the revival of those particular canons and deprecatory remarks in the ecclesiastical councils and writings of a later period of the middle ages, shows that the existence of the evil had continued unabated. There was an African council in the year 381, from which Burchardus, who compiled his condensation of ecclesiastical decrees for the use of his own time, professes to derive his provisions against " the festivals which were held with Pagan ceremonies." We are there told that, even on the most sacred of the Christian commemoration days, these rites derived from the Pagans were introduced, and that dancing was prac-

ticed in the open street of so infamous a character,
and accompanied with such lascivious language and
gestures, that the modesty of respectable females was
shocked to a degree that prevented their attendance
at the service in the churches on those days. It is
added that the se Pagan ceremonies were even carried into the churches, and that many of the clergy
took part in them.

It is probable, too, that when Paganism itself had
become an offence against the state, and those who
continued attached to it were exposed to persecution,
they embraced the name of Christians as a cover for
the grossest superstitions, and formed sects who practised the rites of Paganism in their secret conventicles, but were placed by the church among the Christian heresies. In some of these, especially among
those of an early date, the obscene rites and principles of the phallic worship seem to have entered
largely, for, though their opponents probably exaggerated the actual vice carried on under their name,
yet much of it must have had an existence in truth.
It was a mixture of the licence of the vulgar Paganism of antiquity with the wild doctrines of the latter
eastern philosophers. The older orthodox writers
dwell on the details of these libidinous rites. Among
the earliest in date were the Adamiani, or Adamites,
who proscribed marriage, and held that the most per-

fect innocence was consistent only with the community of women. The chose *latibula*, or caverns, for their conventicles, at which both sexes assembled together in perfect nakedness. This sect perhaps continued to exist under different forms, but it was revived among the intellectual vagaries of the fifteenth century, and continued at least to be much talked of till the seventeenth. The doctrine of the munity of women. They chose *latibula*, or caverns, ous sexual intercourse in their meetings, were ascribed by the early Christian controversialists to several sects, such as the followers of Florian, and of Carpocratian, who were accused of putting out the lamps in their churches at the end of the evening service, and indulging in sexual intercourse indiscriminately; the Nicolaitæ, who held their wives in common; the Ebionei; and especially the Gnostics, or followers of Basilides, and the Manichæans. The Nicolaites held that the only way to salvation lay through frequent intercourse between the sexes.[1] Epiphanius speaks of a sect who sacrificed a child in their secret rites by pricking it with brazen pins, and then offering its blood.[2] The Gnostics were accused of eating human flesh as well as of lasciviousness, and they also are said to have held their women in

[1] Epiphanii *Panarium*, vol. i, p. 72.
[2] Epiphanius, vol. i, p. 416.

common, and taught that it was a duty to prostitute their wives to their guests.[1] Théy knew their fellow sectarians by a secret sign, which consisted in tickling the palm of the hand with the finger in a peculiar manner. The sign having been recognized, mutual confidence was established, and the stranger was invited to supper; after they had eaten their fill, the husband removed from the side of his wife, and said to her, " Go, exhibit charity to our guest," which was the signal for those further scenes of hospitality. This account is given us by St. Epiphanius, bishop of Constantia. We are told further of rites practiced by the Gnostics, which were still more disgusting, for they were said, after these libidinous scenes, to offer and administer the *semen virile* as their sacrament.[2] A similar practice is described as existing among women in the middle ages for the purpose of securing the love of their husbands, and was perhaps derived from the Gnostics and Manichæans, whose doctrines, brought from the East, appear to have spread themselves extensively into Western Europe.

Of these doctrines, however, we have no traces at

---

[1] On the secret worship and character of the Gnostics, see Epiphanii *Panarium*, vol. i, pp. 84—102.

[2] See details on this subject in Epiphanii *Panarium*, ib. Conf. Prædestinati *Adversus Haeres.*, lib. i, c. 46, where the same thing is said of the Manichæans.

least until the eleventh century, when a great intellectual agitation began in Western Europe, which brought to the surface of society a multitude of strange creeds and strange theories. The popular worship displayed in the great annual festivals, and the equally popular local *fêtes,* urban or rural, were hardly interfered with, or any secret societies belonging to the old worship; the mediæval church did not consider them as heresies, and let them alone. Thus, except now and then a provision of some ecclesiastical council expressed in general terms against superstitions, which was hardly heard at the time and not listened to, they are passed over in silence. But the moment anything under the name of heresy raised its head, the alarm was great. Gnosticism and Manichæism, which had indeed been identical, were the heresies most hated in the Eastern empire, and, as may be supposed, most persecuted; and this persecution was destined to drive them westward. In the seventh century they became modified into a sect which took the name of Paulicians, it is said, from an Armenian enthusiast named Paulus, and they seem to have still further provoked the hatred of the church by making themselves, in their own interests, the advocates of freedom of thought and of ecclesiastical reform. If history be to be believed, their Christian feelings cannot have been very strong, for, unable to resist persecution within the empire, they retired into the territory held by the Saracens, and united with the enemies of the Cross in making war upon the Christian Greeks. Others sought refuge in the country of the Bulgarians, who had very generally embraced their doctrines, which soon spread thence westward. In their progress through Germany to France they were known best as Bulgarians, from the name of the country whence they came; in their way through Italy they retained their name of Paulicians, corrupted in the Latin of that period of the middle ages into *Populicani, Poplicani, Publicani,* &c; and, in French, into *Popelican, Poblican, Policien,* and various other forms which it is unnecessary to enumerate. They began to cause alarm in France at the beginning of t!.e eleventh century, in the reign of king Robert, when, under the name of Popelicans, they had established themselves in the diocese of Orleans, in which city a council was held against them in 1022, and thirteen individuals were condemned to be burnt. The name appears to have lasted into the thirteenth century, but the name of Bulgarians became more permanent, and, in its French form of *Bolgres, Bougres,* or *Bogres,* became the popular name for heretics in general. With these heresies, through the more sensual parts of Gnosticism and Manichæism, there appears to be left hardly room for

doubt that the ancient phallic worship, probably
somwhat modified, and under the shadow of secret
rites, was imported into Western Europe; for, if we
make allowance for the willing exaggerations of religious hatred, and consequent popular prejudice, the
general conviction that these sectarians had rites and
practices of a licentious character appears too strong
to be entirely disregarded, nor does it present anything contrary to what we know of the state of mediæval society, or to the facts which have already been
brought forward in the present essay. These early
sects apear to have professed doctrines rather closely
resembling modern communism, including, like those
of their earlier sectarian predecessors, the community
of women; and this community naturally implies the
abolition of distinctive affinities. One of the writers
against the mediæval heretics assures us that there
were "many professed Christians, both men and
women, who feared no more to go to their sister, or
son or daughter, or brother, or nephew or niece, or
kin or relation, than to their own wife or husband."
They were accused, beyond this, of indulging in unnatural vices, and this charge was so generally believed, that the name of Bulgarus, or heretic, became
equivalent with Sodomite, and hence came the modern French word *bougre,* and its English representatives.

In the course of the eleventh century the sectarians appeared in Italy under the name of Patarini, Paterini, or Patrini, which is said to have been taken from an old quarter of the city of Milan named Pataria, in which they first held their assemblies. A contemporary Englishman, Walter Mapes, gives us a singular account of the Paterini and their secret rites. Some apostates from this heresy, he tells us, had related that, at the first watch of night, they met in their synagogues, closed carefully the doors and windows, and waited in silence, until a black cat of extraordinary bigness descended among them by a rope, and that, as soon as they saw this strange animal, they put out the lights, and muttering through their teeth instead of singing their hymns, felt their way to this object of their worship, and kissed it, according to their feelings of humility or pride, some on the feet, some under the tail, and others on the genitals, after which each seized upon the nearest person of a different sex, and had carnal intercourse as long as he was able. Their leaders taught them that the most perfect degree of charity was "to do or suffer in this manner whatever a brother or sister might desire and ask," and hence, says Mapes, they were called Paterini, *a patiendo*. Other writers have suggested a different derivation, but the one first given appears to be that most generally accepted. The different sects or congregations in Italy and the south, indeed, appear generally to have taken their names from the towns in which they had their seats or head-quarters. Thus, those who were seated at Bagnols, in the department of the Gard, in the south of France, were called by the Latin writers Bagnolenses; the same writers give the name of Concordenses, or Concorezenses, to the heretics of Concordia in Lombardy; and the city of Albi, now the capital of the department of the Tarn, gave its name to the sect of the Albigenses, or Albigeois, the most extensive of them all, which spread over the whole of the south of France. A rich enthusiast of the city of Lyons, named Waldo, who had collected his wealth by mercantile pursuits, and who lived in the twelfth century, sold his property and distributed it among the poor, and he became the head of a sect which possessed poverty as one of its tenets, and received from the name of its founder that of Waldenses or Vaudois. From their posession of voluntary poverty they are sometimes spoken of by the name of *Pauperes de Lugduno,* the paupers of Lyons. Contemporaries speak of the Waldenses as being generally poor ignorant people; yet they spread widely over that part of France and into the valleys of Switzerland, and became so celebrated, that at last nearly all the mediæval heretics were usually classed under the head of Waldenses. Another sect, usually classed with the Waldenses, were called Cathari. The Novatians, a sect which sprang up in the church in the third century, assumed also the name of Cathari, as laying claim to extraordinary purity (καθαροι), but there is no reason for believing that the ancient sect was revived in the Cathari of the later period, or even that the two words are identical. The name of the latter sect is often spelt Gazari, Gazeri, Gaçari, and Chazari; and, as they were more especially a German sect, it is supposed to have been the origin of the German words *Ketzer* and *Ketzerie,* which became the common German terms for a heretic and heresy. It was suggested by Henschenius that this name was derived from the German *Katze* or *Ketze,* a cat, in allusion to the common report that they assembled at night like cats, or ghosts; or the cat may have been an allusion to the belief that in their secret meetings they worshipped that animal. This sect must have been very ignorant and superstitious if it be true which some old writers tell us, that they believed that the sun was a demon, and the moon a female called Heva, and that these two had sexual intercourse every month.[1] Like the other heretical sects, these Cathari were accused of indulging in unnatural vices,

---

[1] Bonacursus, *Vita Haereticornm,* in D'Achery, *Spicilegium,* tom. i, p. 209. This book is considered to have been written about the year 1190.

and the German words *Ketzerie* and *Ketzer* were eventually used to signify sodomy and a sodomite, as well as heresy and a heretic.

The Waldenses generally, taking all the sects which people class under this name, including also the older Bulgari and Publicani, were charged with holding secret meetings, at which the devil appeared to them in the shape, according to some, of a goat, whom they worshipped by offering the kiss *in ano,* after which they indulged in promiscuous sexual intercourse. Some believed that they were conveyed to these meetings by unearthly means. The English chronicler, Ralph de Coggeshall, tells a strange story of the means of locomotion possessed by these heretics. In the city of Rheims, in France, in the time of St. Louis, a handsome young woman was charged with heresy, and carried before the archbishop, in whose presence she avowed her opinions, and confessed that she had received them from a certain old woman of that city. The old woman was then arrested, convicted of being an obstinate heretic, and condemned to the stake. When they were preparing to carry her out to the fire, she suddenly turned to the judges and said, "Do you think that you are able to burn me in your fire? I care neither for it nor for you!" And taking a ball of thread, she threw it out at a large window by which she was standing, holding the end of the thread in her hands, and exclaiming, "Take it!" (*recipe*).

In an instant, in the sight of all who were there, the old woman was lifted from the ground, and, following the ball of thread, was carried into the air nobody knew where; and the archbishop's officers burnt the young woman in her place.[1] It was the belief of most of the old sects of this class, as well as of the more ancient Pagans from whom they were derived, that those who were fully initiated into their most secret mysteries became endowed with powers and faculties above those possessed by ordinary individuals. A list of the errors of the Waldenses, printed in the *Reliquiæ Antiquæ,* from an English manuscript, enumerates among them that they met to indulge in promiscuous sexual intercourse, and held perverse doctrines in accordance with it; that, in some parts, the devil appeared to them in the form of a cat, and that each kissed him under the tail; and that in other parts they rode to the place of meeting upon a staff anointed with a certain unguent, and were conveyed thither in a moment of time. The writer adds that,

---

[1] Radulphus Cogeshalenfis, in the *Amplissima Collectio* of Martene and Durand. On the offences with which the different sects comprised under the name of Waldenses were charged, see Gretser's *Scriptores contra Sectam Waldensium,* which will be found in the twelfth volume of his works, Bonacursus, *Vita Haereticorum,* in the first volume of D'Achery's *Spicilegium,* and the work of a Carthusian monk in Martene and Durand, *Amplissima Collectio,* vol. vi, col. 57 et seq.

---

in the parts where he lived, these practices had not been known to exist for a long time.[1]

Our old chroniclers exult over the small success which attended the efforts of these heretics from France and the South to introduce themselves into our island.[2] These sects, with secret and obscene rites, appear, indeed, to have found most favour among the peoples who spoke a dialect derived from the Latin, and this we might naturally be led to expect, for the fact of the preservation of the Latin tongue is itself a proof of the greater force of the Roman element in the society, that from which these secret rites appear to have been chiefly derived. It is a curious circumstance, in connection with this subject, that the popular oaths and exclamations among the people speaking the languages derived from the Romans are almost all composed of the names of the objects of this phallic worship, an entire contrast to the practice of the Teutonic tribes—the vulgar oaths of the people speaking Neo-Latin dialects are obscene, those of the German race are profane. We have seen how the women of Antwerp, who, though perhaps they did not speak the Roman dialect, appear to have been much influenced by Roman sentiments, made their

---

[1] Wright and Halliwell, *Reliquæ Antiquae*, vol. i, p. 247.

[2] See, for example, Guil, Neubrigensis, *De Rebus Anglicis*, lib. ii, c. 13, and Walter Mapes, *de Nugis Curialium*, p. 62.

appeal to their genius Ters. When a Spaniard is irritated or suddenly excited, he exclaims, *Carajo!* (the virile member) or *Cojones!* (the testicles). An Italian, under similar circumstances, uses the exclamation *Cazzo!* (the virile member). The Frenchman apostrophizes the act, *Foutre!* The female member, *coño* with the Spaniard, *conno* with the Italian, and *con* with the Frechman, was and is used more generally as an expression of contempt, which is also the case with the testicles, *couillons,* in French—those who have had experience in the old days of " diligence " travelling will remember how usual it was for the driver, when the horses would not go quick enough, to address the leader in such terms as, " *Va, donc, vieux con!* " We have no such words used in this manner in the Germanic languages, with the exception, perhaps, of the German *Potz!* and *Potztausend!* and the English equivalent, *Pox!* which last is gone quite out of use. There was an attempt among the fashionables of our Elizabethan age of literature, to introduce the Italian *cazzo* under the form of *catso,* and the French *foutre* under that of *foutra,* but these were mere affectations of a moment, and were so little in accord with our national sentiments that they soon disappeared.

The earliest accounts of a sect which held secret meetings for celebrating obscene rites is found in

France. It appears that, early in the eleventh century, there was in the city of Orleans a society consisting of members of both sexes, who assembled at
certain times in a house there, for the purposes which
are described rather fully in a document found in
the cartulary of the abbey of St. Père at Chartres. As
there stated, they went to the meeting, each carrying
in the hand a lighted lamp, and they began by chaunt-
ing the names of demons in the manner of a litany,
until a demon suddenly descended among them in the
form of an animal. This was no sooner seen, than
they all extinguished their lamps, and each man took
the first female he put his hand upon, and had sexual
intercourse with her, without regard if she were his
mother, or his sister, or a consecrated nun; and this
intercourse, we are told, was looked upon by them
as an act of holiness and religion. The child which
was the fruit of this intercourse was taken on the
eighth day and purified by fire, " in the manner of
the ancient Pagans,"—so says the contemporary
writer of this document,—it was burnt to ashes in a
large fire made for that purpose. The ashes were
collected with great reverence, and preserved, to be
administered to members of the society who were dy-
ing, just as good Christians received the viaticum. It
is added that there was such a virtue in these ashes,
that an individual who had once tasted them would

hardly ever after be able to turn his mind from that heresy and take the path of truth.

Whatever degree of truth there may have been in this story, it must have been greatly exaggerated; but the conviction of the existence of secret societies of this character during the middle ages appears to have been so strong and so generally held, that we must hesitate in rejecting it. Perhaps we may take the leaden tokens already described, and represented in one of our plates,[1] as evidence of the existence of such societies, for these curious objects appear to admit of no other satisfactory explanation than that of having been in use in secret clubs of a very impure character.

It has been already remarked that people soon seized upon accusations of this kind as excuses for persecution, religious and political, and we meet with a curious example in the earlier half of the thirteenth century. The district of Steding, in the north of Germany, now known as Oldenburg, was at the beginning of the thirteenth century inhabited by a people who lived in sturdy independence, but the archbishops of Bremen seem to have claimed some sort of feudal superiority over them, which they resisted by force. The archbishop, in revenge, declared them

[1] See before, p. 60, and Plate ix.

heretics, and proclaimed a crusade against them. Crusades against heretics were then in fashion, for it was just at the time of the great war against the Albigeois. The Stedingers maintained their independence successfully for some years. In 1232 and 1233, the pope issued two bulls against the offending Stedingers, in both of which he charges them with various heathen and magical practices, but in the second he enters more fully into details. These Stedingers, the pope (Gregory IX.) tells us, performed the following ceremonies at the initiation of a new convert into their sect. When the novice was introduced, a toad presented itself, which all who were present kissed, some on the posteriors, and others on the mouth, when they drew its tongue and spittle into their own mouths. Sometimes this toad appeared of only the natural size, but sometimes it was as big as a goose or duck, and often its size was that of an oven. As the novice proceeded, he encountered a man who was extraordinarily pale, with large black eyes, and whose body was so wasted that his flesh seemed to be all gone, leaving nothing but the skin hanging on his bones. The novice kissed this personage, and found him as cold as ice; and after this kiss all traces of the Catholic faith vanished from his heart. Then they all sat down to a banquet; and when this was over, there stepped out of a statue, which stood in their place of meeting, a black cat, as large as a moderate sized dog, which advanced backwards to them, with its tail turned up. The novice first, then the master, and then all the others in their turns, kissed the cat under the tail, and then returned to their places, where they remained in silence, with their heads inclined towards the cat. Then the master suddenly pronounced the words " Spare us! " which he addressed to the next in order; and the third answered, " We know it, lord; " and a fourth added, " We ought to obey." At the close of this ceremony the lights were extinguished, and each man took the first woman who came to hand, and had carnal intercourse with her. When this was over, the candles were again lighted, and the performers resumed their places. Then out of a dark corner of the room came a man, the upper part of whom, above the loins, was bright and radiant as the sun, and illuminated the whole room, while his lower parts were rough and hairy like a cat. The master then tore off a bit of the garment of the novice, and said to the shining personage, " Master, this is given to me, and I give it again to thee." The master replied, "Thou hast served me well, and thou wilt serve me more and better; what thou hast given me I give unto thy keeping." When he had said this, the shining man vanished, and the meeting broke up.

Such were the secret ceremonies of the Stedingers, according to the deliberate statement of Pope Gregory IX, who also charges them with offering direct worship to Lucifer.[1]

But the most remarkable, and at the same time the most celebrated, affair in which these accusations of secret and obscene ceremonies were brought to bear, was that of the trial and dissolution of the order of the knights templars. The charges against the knights templars were not heard of for the first time at the period of their dissolution, but for many years it had been whispered abroad that they had secret opinions and practices of an objectionable character. At length the wealth of the order, which was very great in France, excited the cupidity of King Philippe IV, and it was resolved to proceed against them, and despoil them of their possessions. The grounds for these proceedings were furnished by two templars, one a Gascon, the other an Italian, who were evidently men of bad character, and who, having been imprisoned for some offence or offences, made a confession of the secret practices of their order, and upon these confessions certain articles of accusation were drawn up. These appear to have

---

[1] Baronius, *Annales Ecclesiastici*, tom. xxi, p. 89, where the two bulls are printed, and where the details of the history of the Stedingers will be found.

been enlarged afterwards. In 1307, Jacques de Molay, the grand master of the order, was treacherously allured to Paris by the king, and there seized and thrown into prison. Others, similarly committed to prison in all parts of the kingdom, were examined individually on the charges urged against them, and many confessed, while others obstinately denied the whole. Amongst these charges were the following: I. That on the admission of a new member of the order, after having taken the oath of obedience, he was obliged to deny Christ, and to spit, and sometimes also to trample, upon the cross; 2. That they then received the kiss of the templar, who officiated as receiver, on the mouth, and afterwards were obliged to kiss him *in ano,* on the navel, and sometimes on the generative member; 3. That, in despite of the Saviour, they sometimes worshipped a cat, which appeared amongst them in their secret conclave; 4. That they practised unnatural vice together; 5. That they had idols in their different provinces; in the form of a head, having sometimes three faces, sometimes two, or only one, and sometimes a bare skull, which they called their saviour, and believed its influence to be exerted in making them rich, and in making flowers grow and the earth germinate; and 6. That they always wore about their bodies a cord which had been rubbed against the head, and which served for their protection.[1]

The ceremonies attending the reception into the order were so universally acknowledged, and are described in terms which have so much the appearance of truthfulness, that we can hardly altogether disbelieve in them. The denial was to be repeated thrice, no doubt in imitation of St. Peter. It appears to have been considered as a trial of the strength of the obedience they had just sworn to the order, and they all pleaded that they had obeyed with reluctance, that they had denied with the mouth but not with the heart; and that they had intentionally spit beside the cross and not upon it. In one instance the cross was of silver, but it was more commonly of brass, and still more frequently of wood; on one occasion the cross painted in a missal was used, and the cross on the templar's mantle often served the purpose. When one Nicholas de Compiegne protested against these two acts, all the templars who were present told him that he must do them, for it was the custom of the order.[2] Baldwin de St. Just at first refused, but the receptor warned him that if he persisted in his refusal, it would be the worse for him *(aliter male accideret sibi)*, and then "he was so

---

[1] *Procès des Templiers*, edited by M. Michelet, vol. 1, pp. 90-92.
[2] *Procès des Templiers*, ii, 418.

much alarmed that his hair stood on end." Jacques
de Trecis said that he did it under fear, because his
receptor stood by with a great naked sword in his
hand.[1] Another, Geoffrey de Thatan, having similarly refused, his receptor told him that they were
" points of the order," and that if he did not comply,
"he should be put in such a place that he would
never see his own feet." And another who refused
to utter the words of denial was thrown into prison
and kept there until vespers, and when he saw that
he was in peril of death, he yielded, and did whatever
the receptor required of him, but he adds that he was
so troubled and frightened that he had forgotten
whether he spat on the cross or not. Gui de la
Roche, a presbyter of the diocese of Limoges, said
that he uttered the denial with great weeping.
Another, when he denied Christ, "was all stupified
and troubled, and it seemed as if he were enchanted,
not knowing what counsel to take, as they threatened
him heavily if he did not do it." When Etienne de
Dijon similarly refused to deny his Saviour, the preceptor told him that he must do it because he had
sworn to obey his orders, and then " he denied with
his mouth," he said, "but not with his heart; and he
did this with great grief," and he adds that when it

---

[1] *Procès*, 1, 254.

was done, he was so conscience-struck that "he wished he had been outside at his liberty, even though it had been with the loss of one of his arms." When Odo de Dompierre, with great reluctance, at length spat on the cross, he said that he did it with such bitterness of heart that he would rather have had his two thighs broken. Michelet, in the account of the proceedings against the templars in his "History of France," offers an ingenious explanation of these ceremonies of initiation which gives them a typical meaning. He imagines that they were borrowed from the figurative mysteries and rites of the early Church, and supposes that, in this spirit, the candidate for admission into the order was first presented as a sinner and renegade, in which character, after the example of Peter, he was made to deny Christ. This denial, he suggests, was a sort of pantomime in which the novice expressed his reprobate state by spitting on the cross; after which he was stripped of his profane clothing, received, through the kiss of the order, into a higher state of faith, and clothed with the garb of its holiness. If this were the case, the true meaning of the performance must have been very soon forgotten.

This was especially the case with the kiss. According to the articles of accusation, one of the ceremonies of initiation required the novice to kiss the

receiver on the mouth, on the *anus,* or the end of the
spine, on the navel, and on the *virga virilis.* The
last is not mentioned in the examinations, but the
others are described by so many of the witnesses that
we cannot doubt of their truth. From the depositions
of many of the templars examined, it would appear
that the usual order was to kiss the receptor first *in
ano,* next on the navel, and then on the mouth.[1] The
first of these was an act which would, of course, be
repulsive to most people, and the practice arose gradually of only kissing the end of the spine, or, as it was
called in mediæval Latin, *in anca.* Bertrand de
Somorens, of the diocese of Amiens, describing a
reception at which more than one new member was
admitted, says that the receiver next told them that
they must kiss him *in ano;* but, instead of kissing
him there, they lifted up his clothes and kissed him
on the spine. The receptor, it appears, had the power
of remitting this kiss when he judged there was a
sufficient reason. Etienne de Dijon, a presbyter of
the diocese of Langres, said that, when he was admitted into the order, the preceptor told him that
he ought, "according to the observances of the order," to kiss his receiver *in ano,* but that in consideration of his being a presbyter, he would spare him
and remit this kiss. Pierre de Grumenil, also a

[1] See the *Procès,* ii. 286, 362, 364.

presbyter, when called upon to perform this act, refused, and was allowed to kiss his receiver on the navel only. A presbyter named Ado de Dompierre was excused for the same reason,[1] as well as many others. Another templar, named Pierre de Lanhiac, said that, at his reception into the order, his receptor told him that he must kiss him *in ano*, because that was one of the points of the order, but that, at the earnest supplication of his uncle, who was present, and must therefore have been a knight of the order, he obtained a remission of this kiss.

Another charge against the templars was still more disgusting. It was said that they proscribed all intercourse with women, and one of the men examined stated, which was also confessed by others, that his receptor told him that, from that hour, he was never to enter a house in which a woman lay in labour, nor to take part as godfather at the baptism of any child, but he added that he had broken his oath, for he had assisted at the baptism of several children while still in the order, which he had left about a year before the seizure of the templars, for the love of a woman of whom he had become enamoured. On the other hand, those who replied to the interrogatory of the king's officers in this process, were all but unanimous in the avowal that on entering the order

---

[1] *Procès*, 1, 307.

they received the permission to commit sodomy amongst themselves. Two or three professed not to have understood this injunction in a bad sense, but to have supposed that it only meant that, when the brethren were short of beds, each was to be ready to lend half of his bed to his fellow. One of them, named Gillet de Encraye, said that he at first supposed it to be meant innocently, but that his receptor immediately undeceived him, by repeating it in less covert terms, at which he was himself so horrified that he wished himself far away from the chapel in which the ceremony took place. A great number of templars stated that, after the kisses of initiation, they were informed that if they felt moved by natural heat, they might call any one of the brethren to their relief, and that they ought to relieve their brethren when appealed to under the same circumstances. This appears to have been the most common form of the injunction. In one or two instances the receiver is described as adding that this was an act of contempt towards the other sex, which may perhaps be considered as showing that the ceremony was derived from some of the mysteries of the strange sects which appeared in the earlier ages of Christianity. Jean de St. Loup, who held the office of master of the house of templars at Soisiac, said that, on his reception into the order, he received the injunction not to have intercourse with women, but, if he could not persevere in continence, he might have the same intercourse with men; and others were told that it would "be better to satisfy their lust among themselves, whereby the order would escape evil report, than if they went to women." But although the almost unanimity of the confessions leave hardly room for a doubt that such injunctions were given, yet on the other hand they are equally unanimous in denying that these injunctions were carried into practice. Almost every templar, as the questions were put to him, after admitting that he was told that he might indulge in such vice with the other brethren, asserted that he had never done this, and that he had never been asked to do so by any of them. Theobald de Taverniac, whose name tells us that he came from the south, denied indignantly the existence of such a vice among their order but in terms which themselves told not very much in favour of the morality of the templars in other respects. He said that, " as to the crime of sodomy," he believed the charge to be totally untrue, "because they could have very handsome and elegant women when they liked, and that they did have them frequently when they were rich and powerful enough to afford it, and that on this account he and other brothers of the order were removed from their houses, as he said." We have an implied acknowledgment that the templars did not entirely neglect the other sex in a statement quoted by Du Puy that, if a child were born from the intercourse between a templar and a virgin, they roasted it, and made an unguent of its fat, with which they anointed their idol. Those who confessed to the existence of the vice were so few, and their evidence so indefinite or indirect, that they are deserving of no consideration. One had heard that some brethren beyond the sea had committed unnatural vices.[1] Another, Hugh de Faure, had heard say that two brothers of the order, dwelling in the Chateau Pelerin, had been charged with sodomy; that, when this reached the ears of the master, he gave orders for their arrest, and that one had been killed in the attempt to escape, while the other was taken and imprisoned for life. Peter Brocart, a templar of Paris, declared that one of the order, one night, called him and committed sodomy with him; adding that he had not refused, because he considered himself bound to obedience by the rules of the order.[2] The evidence is decidedly strong against the prevalence of such a vice among the templars, and the alleged permission was perhaps a mere form of words, which concealed some occult meaning unknown to the mass of the

[1] *Procès*, ii, 213.
[2] *Procès*, ii, 294.

templars themselves. We are not inclined to reject altogether the theory of the baron von Hammer-Pürgstall, that the templars had adopted some of the mysterious tenets of the eastern Gnostics.

In regard to the secret idolatry with which the templars were charged, it is a subject involved in great obscurity. The cat is but little spoken of in the depositions. Some Italian knights confessed that they had been present at a secret chapter of twelve knights held at Brindisi, when a grey cat suddenly appeared amongst them, and they worshipped it. At Nismes, some templars declared that they had been present at a chapter at Montpellier, when the demon appeared to them in the form of a cat, and promised them worldly prosperity, but they appear to have been visionaries not to be trusted, for they stated that at the same time devils appeared in the shape of women. An English templar, examined in London, deposed that in England they did not adore the cat, or the idol, but that he had heard it positively stated that the cat and the idol were worshipped by the templars in parts beyond sea. A solitary Freshman, examined in Paris, Gillet de Encreyo, spoke of the cat, and said that he had heard, but had forgotten who were his informants, and did not believe them, that beyond sea a certain cat had appeared to the templars in their battles. The cat belongs to a lower class of popular superstitions, perhaps, than that of the templars.

This, however, was not the case with the idol, which was generally described as the figure of a human head, and appears only to have been shown in the more secret chapter meetings on particular occasions. Many of the templars examined before the commissioners, said that they had heard this idol head spoken of as existing in the order, and others deposed to having seen it. It was generally described as being about the natural size of a man's head, with a very fierce-looking face and a beard, the latter sometimes white. Different witnesses varied as to the material of which it was made, and, indeed, in various other particulars, which lead us to suppose that each house of the templars, where the idol existed, had its own head, and that they varied in form. They agreed generally that this head was an object of worship. One templar deposed that he was present at a chapter of the order in Paris, when the head was brought in, but he was unable to describe it at all, for, when he saw it, he was so struck with terror that he hardly knew where he was. Another, Ralph de Gysi, who held the office of receptor for the province of Champagne, said that he had seen the head in many chapters; that, when it was introduced, all present threw themselves on the ground and adored it: and when asked to describe it, he said, on his oath, that its countenance was so terrible, that it seemed to him to be the figure of a demon—using the French word *un maufé,* and that as often as he saw it, so great a fear took possession of him, that he could hardly look upon it without fear and trembling. Jean Taylafer said that, at his reception into the order, his attention was directed to a head upon the altar in the chapel, which he was told he must worship; he described it as of the natural size of a mans head, but could not describe it more particularly, except that he thought it was of a reddish colour.[1] Raynerus de Larchent saw the head twice in a chapter, especially once in Paris, where it had a beard, and they adored and kissed it, and called it their saviour. Guillermus de Herbaleyo saw the head with its beard, at two chapters. He thought it was of silver gilt, and wood inside. He " saw the brethren adore it, and he went through the form of adoring it himself, but he did it not in his heart." According to one witness, Deodatus Jaffet, a knight from the south of France who had been received at Pedenat, the receptor showed him a head, or idol, which appeared to have three faces, and said to him, " You must adore this as your saviour, and the saviour of the order of the temple," and he added that he was made to worship the idol,

---

[1] *Procès,* i, 190.

saying, "Blessed be he who shall save my soul!" Another deponent gave a very similar account. Another knight of the order, Hugo de Paraudo, said that, in a chapter at Montpellier, he had both seen, held, and felt, the idol or head, and that he and the other brothers adored it but he, like the others, pleaded that he did not adore it in his heart. He described it as supported on four feet, two before and two behind.[1] Guillaume de Arrablay, the king's almoner *(eleemosynarius regius)*, said that in the chapter at which he was received, a head made of silver was placed on the altar, and adored by those who formed the chapter; he was told that it was the head of one of the eleven thousand virgins, and had always believed this to be the case, until after the arrest of the order, when, hearing all that was said on the matter, he " suspected " that it was the idol; and he adds in his deposition that it seemed to him to have two faces, a terrible look, and a silver beard. It does not appear very clear why he should have taken a head with two faces, a fierce look, and a beard, for one of the eleven thousand virgins, but this is, perhaps, partly explained by the deposition of another witness, Guillaume Pidoye, who had the charge of the relics, &c., belonging to the Temple in Paris, and who produced a head of silver gilt, hav-

---

[1] *Procès,* ii, 363.

---

ing a woman's face, and a small skull, resembling
that of a woman, inside, which was said to be that of
one of the eleven thousand virgins. At the same time
another head was brought forward, having a beard,
and supposed to be that of the idol.[1] Both these
witnesses had no doubt confounded two things.
Pierre Garald, of Mursac, another witness, said that
after he had denied Christ and spitten on the cross,
the receptor drew from his bosom a certain small
image of brass or gold, which appeared to represent
the figure of a woman, and told him that " he must
believe in it, and have faith in it, and that it would
be well for him." Here the idol appears in the form
of a statuette. There was also another account of the
idol, which perhaps refers to some further object of
superstition among the templars. According to one
deponent, it was an old skin embalmed, with bright
carbuncles for eyes, which shone like the light of
heaven. Others said that it was the skin of a man,
but agreed with the others in regard to the carbuncles.[2] In England a minorite friar deposed that
an English knight of the Temple had assured him
that the templars had four principal idols in this
country, one in the sacristy of the Temple in London,
another at Bristelham, a third at Brueria (Bruern in

---

[1] *Procès,* ii, 218.
[2] Du Puy, *Hist. des Templ.,* pp. 22, 24.

Lincolnshire), and the fourth at some place beyond the Humber.[1]

Another piece of information relating to this "idol," which has been the subject of considerable discussion among modern writers, was elicited from the examination of some knights from the south. Gauserand de Montpesant, a knight of Provence, said that their superior showed him an idol made in the form of Baffomet; another, named Raymond Rubei, described it as a wooden head, on which the figure of Baphomet was painted, and adds, "that he worshipped it by kissing its feet, and exclaiming, 'Yalla,' which was," he says, "*verbum Saracenorum,*" a word taken from the Saracens.[2] A templar of Florence declared that, in the secret chapters of the order, one brother said to the other, showing the idol, "Adore this head—this head is your god and your Mahomet." The word Mahomet was used commonly in the middle ages as a general term for an idol or false god; but some writers have suggested that Baphomet is itself a mere corruption of Mahomet, and suppose that the templars had secretly embraced Mahometanism. A much more remarkable explanation of this word has, however, been proposed, which is, at the least, worthy of very great consideration, especially

[1] Wilkins, *Concil.*, vol. ii, p. 363.
[2] Du Puy, *Hist. des Templiers*, p. 21.

as it comes from so distinguished an orientalist and scholar as the late baron Joseph von Hammer-Pürgstall. It arose partly from the comparison of a number of objects of art, ornamented with figures, and belonging apparently to the thirteenth century. These objects consist chiefly of small images, or statuettes, coffers, and cups.

Von Hammer has described, and given engravings of, twenty-four such images, which it must be acknowledged answer very well to the descriptions of their " idol " given by the templars in their examinations, except only that the templars usually speak of them as of the size of life, and as being merely heads. Most of them have beards, and tolerably fierce countenances. Among those given by Von Hammer are seven which present only a head, and two with two faces, backwards and forwards, as described in some of the depositions. These two appear to be intended for female heads. Altogether Von Hammer has described fifteen cups and goblets, but a much smaller number of coffers. Both cups and coffers are ornamented with extremely curious figures, representing a continuous scene, apparently religious ceremonies of some kind or other, but certainly of an obscene character, all the persons engaged in which are represented naked. It is not a part of our subject to enter into a detailed examination of these mysteries. The most interesting of the coffers described by Von Hammer, which was preserved in the private museum of the duc de Blacas, is of calcarous stone, nine inches long by seven broad, and four and a half deep, with a lid about two inches thick. It was found in Burgundy. On the lid is sculptured a figure, naked, with a head-dress resembling that given to Cybele in ancient monuments, holding up a chain with each hand, and surrounded with various symbols, the sun and moon above, the star and the pentacle below, and under the feet a human skull.[1] The chains are explained by Von Hammer as representing the chains of æons of the Gnostics. On the four sides of the coffer we see a series of figures engaged in the performance of various ceremonies, which are not easily explained, but which Von Hammer considers as belonging to the rites of the Gnostics and Ophians. The offering of a calf figures prominently among these rites, a worship which is said still to exist among the Nossarii, or Nessarenes, the Druses, and other sects in the East. In the middle of the scene on one side, a human skull is seen, raised upon a pole. On another side an androgynous figure is represented as the object of worship of two candidates for initiation, who wear masks apparently of a cat, and whose form of adoration reminds us of the kiss enacted at the initi-

[1] See our plate xiv.

PLATE XIV

PRIAPIC ILLUSTRATIONS FROM OLD BALLADS

ation of the templars.[1] This group reminds us, too, of the pictures of the orgies in the worship of Priapus, as represented on Roman monuments. The second of the coffers in the cabinet of the duc de Blacas was found in Tuscany, and is rather larger than the one just described, but made of the same material, though of a finer grain. The lid of this coffer is lost, but the sides are covered with sculpture of a similar character. A large goblet, or bowl, of marble, in the imperial museum at Vienna, is surrounded by a series of figures of similar character, which are engraved by Von Hammer, who sees in one group of men (who are furnished in the original with prominent phalli) and serpents, a direct allusion to Ophite rites. Next after these comes a group which we have reproduced in our plate,[2] representing a strange figure seated upon an eagle, and accompanied with two of the symbols represented on the coffer found in Burgundy, the sun and moon. The two symbols below are considered by Von Hammer to represent, according to the rude mediæval notions of its form, the womb, or matrix; the fecundating organ is penetrating the one, while the infant is emerging from the other. The last figure in this series, which we have also copied,[3]

---

[1] Plate xv, fig. 1.

[2] Plate xv, fig. 2.

[3] Plate xv, fig. 3.

is identical with that on the lid of the coffer found in Burgundy, but it is distinctly represented as androgynous. We have exactly the same figure on another coffer, in the Vienna museum,[1] with some of the same symbols, the star, pentacle, and human skull. Perhaps, in this last, the beard is intended to show that the figure must be taken as androgynous.

On an impartial comparison we can hardly doubt that these curious objects,—images, coffers, cups, and bowls,—have been intended for use in some secret and mysterious rites, and the arguments by which Von Hammer attempts to show that they belonged to the templars seem at least to be very plausible. Several of the objects represented upon them, even the skull, are alluded to in some of the confessions of the templars, and these evidently only confessed a part of what they knew, or otherwise they were very imperfectly acquainted with the secrets of their order. Perhaps the most secret doctrines and rites were only communicated fully to a small number. There is, however, another circumstance connected with these objects which appears to furnish an almost irresistible confirmation of Von Hammer's theory. Most of them bear inscriptions, written in Arabic, Greek, and Roman characters. The inscriptions on the images appear to be merely proper names, probably those of

[1] Plate xv, fig. 4.

their possessors. But with the coffers and bowls the case is different, for they contain a nearly uniform inscription in Arabic characters, which, according to the interpretation given by Von Hammer, contains a religious formula. The Arabic characters, he says, have been copied by a European, and not very skilful, carver, who did not understand them, from an Eastern original, and the inscriptions contain corruptions and errors which either arose from this circumstance, or, as Von Hammer suggests, may have been introduced designedly, for the purpose of concealing the meaning from the uninitiated. A good example of this inscription surrounds the lid of the coffer found in Burgundy, and is interpreted as follows by Von Hammer, who regards it as a sort of parody on the *Cantate laudes Domini.* In fact, the word under the feet of the figure, between them and the skull, is nothing more than the Latin *cantate* expressed in Arabic letters. The words with which this *Cantate* begins are written above the head of the figure, and are read by Von Hammer as *Fah la Sidna,* which is more correctly *Fella Sidna,* i. e. O God, our Lord! The formula itself, to which this is an introduction, commences on the right side, and the first part of it reads *Houvè Mete Zonar feseba* (or *sebaa*) *B. Mounkir teaala tiz.* There is no such word in Arabic as *mete,* and Von Hammer considers it to be

simply the Greek word μῆτις, wisdom, a personifica-
tion in what we may perhaps call the Gnostic mythology answering to the Sophia of the Ophianites. He
considers that the name Baphomet is derived from
the Greek words Βαφη μητοες, i. e. the baptism· of
Metis, and that in its application it is equivalent with
the name Mete itself. He has further shown, we
think conclusively, that Baphomet, instead of being
a corruption of Mahomet, was a name known among
the Gnostic sects in the East. *Zonar* is not an Arabic
word, and is perhaps only a corruption or error of
the sculptor, but Von Hammer thought it meant a
girdle, and that it alluded to the mysterious girdle of
the templars, of which so much is said in their examinations. The letter *B* is supposed by Von Hammer
to stand here for the name Baphomet, or for that of
Barbalo, one of the most important personages in the
Gnostic mythology. *Mounkir* is the Arabic word for
a person who denies the orthodox faith. The rest of
the formula is given on the other side of the figure,
but as the inscription here presents several corruptions, we will give Von Hammer's translation (in
Latin) of the more correct copy of the formula in-
scribed on the bowl or goblet preserved in the
museum at Vienna. In the Vienna bowl, the formula
of faith is written on a sort of large placard, which
is held up to view by a figure apparently intended for

PLATE XV

"IDOL" OF THE KNIGHTS TEMPLARS

another representation of Mete or Baphomet. Von Hammer translates it:—

"Exaltetur Mete germinans, stirps nostra ego et septem fuere, *tu renegans reditus* ὥρωχτὸς fis."

This still is, it must be confessed, rather mysterious, and, in fact, most of these copies of the formula of faith are more or less defective, but, from a comparison of them, the general form and meaning of the whole is made perfectly clear. This may be translated, " Let Mete be exalted, who causes things to bud and blossom! he is our root; it (the root) is one and seven; abjure (the faith), and abandon thyself to all pleasures." The number seven is said to refer to the seven archons of the Gnostic creed.

There are certainly several points in this formula which present at least a singular coincidence with the statements made in the examinations of the templars. In the first place the invocation which precedes the formula, Yalla (Jah la), agrees exactly with the statement of Raymond Rubei, one of the Provencal templars that when the superior exhibited the idol, or figure of Baphomet, he kissed it and exclaimed " Yalla! " which he calls " a word of the Saracens," i. e. Arabic.[1] It is evident that, in this case, the witness not only knew the word, but that he knew to what language it belonged. Again, the epithet *germi-*

---

[1] Du Puy, *Hist. des Templiers*, p. 94.

nans, applied to Mete, or Baphomet, is in accord with the statement in the formal list of articles of accusation against the templars, that they worshipped their idol because " it made the trees to flourish and the earth to germinate." The abjuration of the formula on the monuments seems to be identical with the denial in the initiation of novices to the order of the Temple; and it may be added, that the closing words of the formula involve in the original an idea more obscene than is expressed in the translation, an allusion to the unnatural vice in which the templars are stated to have received permission to indulge. There is another curious statement in the examinations which seems to point directly to our images and coffers—one of the English witnesses under examination, named John de Donington, who had left the order and become a friar at Salisbury, said that an old templar had assured him that " some templars carried such idols in their coffers." They seem to have been treasured up for the same reason as the mandrake, for one article in the articles against the templars is that they worshipped their idol because " it could make them rich, and that it had brought all their great wealth to the order."

The two other classes of what the Baron Von Hammer supposed to be relics of the secret worship of the templars, appear to us to be much less satisfactorily explained. These are sculptures on old churches, and coins or medals. Such sculptures are found, according to Von Hammer, on the churches of Schöngraber, Waltendorf, and Bercktoldorf, in Austria; in that of Deutschaltenburg, and in the ruins of that of Postyén, in Hungary; and in those of Murau, Prague, and Egra, in Bohemia. To these examples we are to add the sculptures of the church of Montmorillon, in Poitou, some of which have been engraved by Montfaucon,[1] and those of the church of Ste. Croix, in Bordeaux. We have already [2] remarked the rather frequent prevalence of subjects more or less obscene in the sculptures which ornament early churches, and suggested that they may be explained in some degree by the tone given to society by the existence of this priapic worship; but we are not inclined to agree with Von Hammer's explanation of them, or to think that they have any connection with the templars. We can easily understand the existence of such direct allusions on coffers or other objects intended to be concealed, or at least kept in private; but it is hardly probable that men who held opinions and practised rites the very rumour of which was then so full of danger, would proclaim them publicly on the walls of their buildings, for the wall

---

[1] Montfaucon, *Antiquité Expliquée*, Suppl. tom. ii, plate 59.
[2] See before, p. 139.

151

of a church was then, perhaps, the most effectual
medium of publication. The question of the supposed templar medals is very obscure. Von Hammer
has engraved a certain number of these objects, which
present various singular subjects on the obverse,
sometimes with a cross on the reverse, and sometimes
bracteate. Antiquaries have given the name of abbey
tokens to a rather numerous class of such medals,
the use of which is still very uncertain, although
there appears to be little doubt of its being of a
religious character. Some have supposed that they
were distributed to those who attended at certain
sacraments or rites of the Church, who could thus,
when called up, prove by the number of their tokens,
the greater or less regularity of their attendance.
Whether this were the case or not, it is certain that
the burlesque and other societies of the middle ages,
such as the feast of fools, parodied these " tokens,"
and had burlesque medals, in lead and sometimes in
other metals, which were perhaps used for a similar
purpose. We have already spoken more than once
of obscene medals, and have engraved specimens of
them, which were perhaps used in secret societies derived from, or founded upon, the ancient phallic
worship. It is not at all improbable that the templars may have employed similar medals, and that
those would contain allusions to the rites in which

they were employed. The medals published by Von Hammer are said to have been found chiefly on the sites of settlements of the order of the Temple. However, the comparison of facts stated in the confessions of many of the templars, as preserved in the official reports, with the images and sculptured cups and coffers given by Von Hammer-Pürgstall, lead to the conclusion that there is truth in the explanation he gives of the latter, and that the templars, or at least some of them, had secretly adopted a form of the rites of Gnosticism, which was itself founded upon the phallic worship of the ancients. An English templar, Stephen de Staplebridge, acknowledged that "there were two 'professions' in the order of the Temple, the first lawful and good, the second contrary to the faith." He had been admitted to the first of these when he first entered the order, eleven years before the time of his examination, but he was only initiated into the second or inner mysteries about a year afterwards; and he gives almost a picturesque description of this second initiation, which occurred in a chapter held at "Dineslee" in Herefordshire. Another English templar, Thomas de Tocci, said that the errors had been brought into England by a French knight of high position in the order.[1]

---

[1] Wilkins, *Concil.*, ii, 387.

We have thus seen in how many various forms the old phallic, or priapic, worship presented itself in the middle ages, and how pertinaciously it held its ground through all the changes and developments of society, until at length we find all the circumstances of the ancient priapic orgies, as well as the mediæval additions, combined in that great and extensive superstition—witchcraft. At all times the initiated were believed to have obtained thereby powers which were not possessed by the uninitiated, and they only were supposed to know the proper forms of invocation of the deities who were the objects of their worship, which deities the Christian teachers invariably transformed into devils. The vows which the people of antiquity addressed to Priapus, those of the middle ages addressed to Satan. The witches' " Sabbath " was simply the last form which the Priapeia and Liberalia assumed in Western Europe, and in its various details all the incidents of those great and licentious orgies of the Romans were reproduced. The Sabbath of the witches does not appear to have formed a part of the Teutonic mythology, but we can trace it from the South through the countries in which the Roman element of society predominated. The incidents of the Sabbath are distinctly traced in Italy as early as the beginning of the fifteenth century, and soon afterwards they are found in the south of France. Towards the middle of that century an individual named Robinet de Vaulx, who had lived the life of a hermit in Burgundy, was arrested, brought to a trial at Langres, and burnt. This man was a native of Artois; he stated that to his knowledge there were a great number of witches in that province, and he not only confessed that he had attended these nocturnal assemblies of the witches, but he gave the names of some inhabitants of Arras whom he had met there. At this time—it was in the year 1459—the chapter general of the Jacobins, or friars preachers, was held at Langres, and among those who attended it was a Jacobin friar named Pierre de Broussart, who held the office of inquisitor of the faith in the city of Arras, and who eagerly listened to the circumstances of Robinet's confession. Among the names mentioned by him as having been present at the witches' meetings, were those of a prostitute named Demiselle, then living at Douai, and a man named Jehan Levite, but who was better known by the nickname of *Abbé de peu de sens* (the abbot of little sense). On Broussart's return to Arras, he caused both these persons to be arrested and brought to that city, where they were thrown into prison. The latter, who was a painter, and a composer and singer of popular songs, had left Arras before Robinet de Vaulx had made his confession, but he was traced to Abbeville, in Ponthieu, and captured there. Confessions were extorted from these persons which compromised others, and a number of individuals were committed to prison in consequence. In the sequel a certain number of them were burnt, after they had been induced to unite in a statement to the following effect. At this time, in this part of France at least, the term Vauderie, or, as it was then written, Vaulderie, was applied to the practice or profession of witchcraft. They said that the place of meeting was commonly a fountain in the wood of Mofflaines, about a league distant from Arras, and that they sometimes went thither on foot. The more usual way of proceeding, however, according to their own account, was this—they took an ointment given to them by the devil, with which they annointed a wooden rod, at the same time rubbing the palms of their hands with it, and then, placing the rod between their legs, they were suddenly carried through the air to the place of assembly. They found there a multitude of people, of both sexes, and of all estates and ranks, even wealthy burghers and nobles—and one of the persons examined declared that he had seen there not only ordinary ecclesiastics, but bishops and even cardinals. They found tables already spread, covered with all sorts of meats, and abundance of wines. A devil presided, usually in the form

of a goat, with the tail of an ape, and a human countenance. Each first did oblation and homage to him
by offering him his or her soul, or, at least some part
of their body, and then, as a mark of adoration,
kissed him on the posteriors. All this time the worshippers held burning torches in their hands. The
abbot of little sense, already mentioned, held the
office of master of the ceremonies at these meetings, and it was his duty to see that the new-comers
duly performed their homage. After this they tram-
pled on the cross, and spit upon it, in despite of
Jesus and of the Holy Trinity, and performed other
profane acts. They then seated themselves at the
tables, and after they had eaten and drunk sufficiently, they rose and joined in a scene of promiscuous intercourse between the sexes, in which the
demon took part, assuming alternately the form of
either sex, according to that of his temporary partner. Other wicked acts followed, and then the devil
preached to them, and enjoined them especially not
to go to church, or hear mass, or touch holy water,
or perform any other of the duties of good Christians.
After this sermon was ended, the meeting was dis-
solved, and they separated and returned to their
several homes.[1]

---

[1] The account of the witch trials at Arras was published in the
supplementary additions to Monstrelet; but the original records
of the proceedings have since been found and printed.

The violence of these witch persecutions at Arras led to a reaction, which, however, was not lasting, and from this time to the end of the century, the fear of witchcraft spread over Italy, France, and Germany, and went on increasing in intensity. It was during this period that witchcraft, in the hands of the more zealous inquisitors, was gradually worked up into a great system, and books of considerable extent were compiled, containing accounts of the various practices of the witches, and directions for proceeding against them. One of the earliest of these writers was a Swiss friar, named John Nider, who held the office of inquisitor in Switzerland, and has devoted one book of his *Formicarium* to witchcraft as it existed in that country. He makes no allusion to the witches' Sabbath, which, therefore, appears then not to have been known among the Swiss. Early in 1489, Ulric Molitor published a treatise on the same subject, under the title of *De Pythonicis Mulieribus*, and in the same year, 1489, appeared the celebrated book, the *Malleus Maleficarum*, or Hammer of Witches, the work of the three inquisitors for Germany, the chief of whom was Jacob Sprenger. This work gives us a complete and very interesting account of witchcraft as it then existed as an article of belief in Germany. The authors discuss various questions connected with it, such as that of the mysterious transport of witches from one place to another, and they decide that this transport was real, and that they were carried bodily through the air. It is remarkable, however, that even the *Malleus Maleficarum* contains no direct allusion to the Sabbath, and we may conclude that even then this great priapic orgie did not form a part of the Germanic creed; it was no doubt brought in there amid the witchcraft mania of the sixteenth century. From the time of the publication of the *Malleus Maleficarum* until the beginning of the seventeenth century, through all parts of Western Europe, the number of books upon sorcery which issued from the press was immense; and we must not forget that a monarch of our own, King James I, shone among the writers on witchcraft.

Three quarters of a century nearly had passed since the time of the *Malleus,* when a Frenchman named Bodin, Latinised into Bodinus, published a rather bulky treatise which became from that time the text-book on witchcraft. The Sabbath is described in this book in all its completeness. It was usually held in a lonely place, and when possible on the summits of mountains or in the solitude of forests. When the witch prepared to attend it, she went to her bedroom, stripped herself naked, and anointed her body with an ointment made for that purpose. She next took a staff, which also in many cases she anointed, and placing it between her legs and uttering a charm, she was carried through the air, in an incredibly short space of time, to the place of meeting. Bodin discusses learnedly the question whether the witches were really carried through the air corporeally or not, he decides it in the affirmative. The Sabbath itself was a great assemblage of witches, of both sexes, and of demons. It was a point of emulation with the visitors to bring new converts with them, and on their arrival they presented these to the demon who presided, and to whom they offered their adoration by the unclean kiss upon his posteriors. They next rendered an account of all the mischief they had perpetrated since the previous meeting, and received reward or reproof according to its amount. The devil, who usually took the form of a goat, next distributed among them powders, unguents, and other articles to be employed in similar evil doings in future. The worshippers now made offerings to the devil, consisting of sheep, or other articles, or, in some cases, of a little bird only, or of a lock of the witches' hair, or of some other equally trifling object. They were then obliged to seal their denial of the Christian faith by trampling on the cross and blaspheming the saints. The devil then, or in the course of the meeting, had sexual intercourse with the new witch, placed his mark upon some concealed part of her body, very commonly in her sexual parts, and gave her a familiar or imp, who was to be at her bidding and assist in the perpetration of evil. All this was what may be called the business of the meeting, and when it was over, they all went to a great banquet, which was set out on tables, and which sometimes consisted of sumptuous viands, but more frequently of loathsome or unsubstantial food, so that the guests often left the meeting as hungry as though they had tasted nothing. After the feast they all rose from the table to dance, and a scene of wild and uproarious revelry followed. The usual dance on this occasion appears to have been the *carole* of the middle ages, which was no doubt the common dance of the peasantry; a party, alternately a male and a female, held each other's hands in a circle, with this peculiarity that, whereas in ordinary life the dancers turned their faces inward into the circle, here they turned them outwards, so that their backs were towards the interior of the circle. It was pretended that this arrangement was designed to prevent them from seeing and recognizing each other; but others supposed that it was a mere caprice of the evil one, who wished to do everything in a form contrary to that in which it was usually done by Christians. Other dances were introduced, of a more violent, and some of them of an obscene, character. The songs, too, which were sung in this orgie were either obscene or vulgarly ridiculous. The music was often drawn from burlesque instruments, such as a stick or a bone for a flute, a horse's skull for a lyre, the trunk of a tree for a drum, and a branch for a trumpet. As they became excited, they became more licentious, and at last they abandoned themselves to indiscriminate sexual intercourse, in which the demons played a very active part. The meeting separated in time to allow the witches, by the same expeditious conveyance which brought them, to reach their homes before the cock crowed.[1]

Such is the account of the Sabbath, as described by Bodin; but we have reviewed it briefly in order to describe this strange scene from the much fuller and more curious narrative of another Frenchman, Pierre de Lancre. This man was a conseiller du roi, or judge in the parliament of Bordeaux, and was joined in 1609 with one of his colleagues in a commission to proceed against persons accused of sorcery in Labourd, a district in the Basque provinces, then celebrated for its witches, and apparently for

---

[1] The first edition of the work of Bodin, *De la Démonomanie des Sorciers*, was published at Paris, in 4to, in 1580. It went through many editions, and was translated into Latin and other languages.

the low state of morality among its inhabitants. It is a wild, and, in many parts, desolate region, the inhabitants of which held to their ancient superstitions with great tenacity. De Lancre, after arguing learnedly on the nature and character of demons, discusses the question why there were so many of them in the country of Labourd, and why the inhabitants of that district were so much addicted to sorcery. The women of the country, he says, were naturally of a lascivious temperament, which was shown even in their manner of dressing, for he describes their head-dress as being singularly indecent, and describes them as commonly exposing their person very immodestly. He adds, that the principal produce of this country consisted of apples, and argues thence, it is not very apparent why, that the women partook of the character of Eve, and yielded more easily to temptation than those of other countries. After having spent four months in dealing out rather severely what was then called " justice " to these ignorant people, the two commissioners returned to Bordeaux, and there De Lancre, deeply struck with what he had seen and heard, betook himself to the study of witchcraft, and in due time produced his great work on the subject, to which he gave the title of *Tableau de l' Inconstance des Mauvais Anges et*

Démons.[1] Pierre de Lancre writes honestly and con-
scientiously, and he evidently believes everything he
has written.   His book is valuable for the great
amount of new information it contains, derived from
the confessions of the witches, and given apparently
in their own words. The second book is devoted entirely to the details of the Sabbath.

It was stated by the witches in their examinations
that, in times back, they had appointed Monday to be
the day, or rather night, of assembly, but that in their
time they had two nights of meeting in the week,
those of Wednesday and Friday.   Although some
stated that they had been carried to the place of meeting in the middle of the day, they mostly agreed in
saying that the hour at which they were carried to
the Sabbath was midnight. The place of assembly
was usually chosen at a spot where roads crossed, but
this was not always the case, for De Lancre tells us
that they were accustomed to hold their Sabbath in
some lonely and wild locality, as in the middle of a
heath, which was selected especially for being far
from the haunts or habitations of man. To this place,
he says, they gave the name of Aquelarre, which he
interprets as meaning *Lane de Bouc,* that is, the heath
of the goat, meaning that it was the place where the

---

[1] 4to. Paris, 1612. A new and improved edition appeared in
1613.

---

goat, the usual form assumed by Satan, convoked his assemblies. And he goes on to express his opinion that these wild places were the original scenes of the Sabbath, though subsequently other places had been often adopted. " For we have heard more than fifty witnesses who assured us that they had been at the Goat's Heath to the Sabbath held on the mountain of La Rhune, sometimes on the open mountain, sometimes in the chapel of the St. Esprit, which is on the top of it, and sometimes in the church of Dordach, which is on the borders of Labourd. At times they held it in private houses, as when we held the trial, in the parish of St. Pé, the Sabbath was held one night in our hotel, called Barbare-nena, and in that of Master —— de Segure, assessor-criminal at Bayonne, who, at the same time when we were there, made a more ample inquisition against certain witches, by an authority of an arrest of the parliament of Bordeaux. Then they went the same night to hold it at the residence of the lord of the place, who is Sieur d'Amou, and in his castle of St. Pé. But we have not found in the whole country of Labourd any other parish but that of St. Pé where the devil held the Sabbath in private houses."

The devil is further described as seeking for his places of meeting, besides the heaths, old decayed houses, and ruins of old castles, especially when they

trunk of a tree, without arms or feet, seated in a chair, with the face of a great and frightful looking man. Others spoke of him as resembling a great goat, with two horns before and two behind, those before turned up in the semblance of a woman's perruque. According to the most common account, De Lancre says he had three horns, the one in the middle giving out a flame, with which he used at the Sabbath to give both light and fire to the witches, some of whom who had candles lit them at his horn, in order to hold them at a mock service of the mass, which was one of the devil's ceremonies. He had also, sometimes, a kind of cap or hat over his horns. "He has before him his member hanging out, which he exhibits always a cubit in length; and he has a great tail behind, with a form of a face under it, with which face he does not utter a word, but it serves only to offer to kiss to those he likes, honouring certain witches of either sex more than the others." The devil, it will be observed, is here represented with the symbol of Priapus. Marie d'Aspilecute, aged nineteen years, who lived at Handaye, deposed that the first time she was presented to the devil she kissed him on this face behind, beneath a great tail, and that she repeated the kiss three times, adding that this face was made like the muzzle of a goat. Others said that he was shaped like a great man, " enveloped in a cloudiness, because

he would not be seen clearly," and that he was all
" flamboyant," and had a face red like an iron coming
out of the furnace. Corneille Brolic, a lad of twelve
years of age, said that when he was first introduced
to him he had the human form, with four horns on
his head, and without arms. He was seated in a
pulpit, with some of the women, who were his favour-
ites, always near him. "And they are all agreed that
it is a great pulpit, which seems to be gilt and very
pompous." Janette d'Abadie, of Siboro, sixteen years
old, said that Satan had a face before and another
behind his head, as they represent the god Janus.
De Lancre had also heard him described as a great
black dog, as a large ox of brass lying down, and as a
natural ox in repose.

Although it was stated that in former times the
devil had usually appeared in the form of a serpent,—another coincidence with the priapic worship,—it appears certain that in the time of De Lancre his favourite form of showing himself was that of
a goat. At the opening of the Sabbath the witches,
male or female, presented formally to the devil those
who had never been at the Sabbath before, and the
women especially brought to him the children whom
they allured to him. The new converts, the novices,
were made to renounce Christ, the Virgin Mary, and
the saints, and they were then re-baptized with mock

ceremonies. They next performed their worship to
the devil by kissing him on the face under the tail, or
otherwise. The young children were taken to the
edge of a stream—for the scene was generally chosen
on the banks of a stream—and white wands were
placed in their hands, and they were entrusted with
the care of the toads which were kept there, and
which were of importance in the subsequent opera-
tions of the witches. The renunciation was frequently
renewed, and in some cases it was required every
time the witch attended the Sabbath. Janette
d'Abadie, a girl of sixteen, said that he made her re-
peatedly go through the ceremony of kissing him
on the face, and afterwards on the navel, then on the
virile member, and then on the posteriors. After re-
baptism, he put his mark on the body of his victim,
in some covered part where it was not likely to be
seen. In women it was often placed on or within the
sexual parts.

De Lancre's account of the proceedings at the Sabbath is very full and curious. He says that it "resembled a fair of merchants mingled together, furious
and in transports, arriving from all parts—a meeting
and mingling of a hundred thousand subjects, sudden and transitory, novel, it is true, but of a frightful
novelty, which offends the eye and sickens you.
Among these same subjects some are real, and others

deceitful and illusory. Some are pleasing (but very little), as are the little bells and melodious instruments of all sorts, which only tickle the ear and do not touch the heart at all, consisting more in noise which amazes and stuns than in harmony which pleases and rejoices, the others displeasing, full of deformity and horror, tending only to desolation, privation, ruin, and destruction, where the persons become brutish and transformed to beasts, losing their speech while they are in this condition, and the beasts, on the contrary, talk, and seem to have more reason than the persons, each being drawn out of his natural character."

The women, according to De Lancre, were the active agents in all this confusion, and had more employment than the men. They rushed about with their hair hanging loose, and their bodies naked; some rubbed with the magical ointment, others not. They arrived at the Sabbath, or went from it, on their errands of mischief, perched on a stick or besom, or carried upon a goat or other animal, with an infant or two behind, and guided or driven on by the devil himself. "And when Satan will transport them into the air (which is an indulgence only to the most superior), he sets them off and launches them up like fired rockets, and they repair to and dart down upon the said place a hundred times more rapidly than an eagle or a kite could dart upon its prey."

These women, on their arrival, reported to Satan all the mischief they had perpetrated. Poison, of all kinds and for all purposes, was there the article most in vogue. Toads were said to form one of its ingredients, and the charge of these animals, while alive, was given to the children whom the witches brought with them to the Sabbath, and to whom, as a sort of ensign of office, little white rods were given, "just such as they give to persons infected with the plague as a mark of their contagion."

The devil was the sovereign master of the assembly, and appeared at it sometimes in the form of a stinking and bearded goat, as one, De Lancre says, which was especially repulsive to mankind. The goat, we know, was dedicated to Priapus. Sometimes he assumed a form, if we clearly understand De Lancre, which presented a confused idea of something between a tree and a man, which is compared, for he becomes rather poetical, to the old decayed cypresses on the summit of a high mountain, or to aged oaks whose heads already bear the marks of approaching decay.

When the devil appeared in human form, that form was horribly ugly and repulsive, with a hoarse voice and an imperious manner. He was seated in a pulpit, which glittered like gold; and at his side sat the queen of the Sabbath, one of the witches whom he had debauched, to whom he chose to give greater honour than to the others, and whom he decked in gay robes, with a crown on her head, to serve as a bait to the ambition of the rest. Candles of pitch, or torches, yielded a false light, which gave people in appearance monstrous forms and frightful faces.

Here you see false fires, through which some of the demons were first passed, and afterwards the witches, without suffering any pain, which, as explained by De Lancre, was intended to teach them not to fear the fire of hell. But we see in these the need-fires, which formed a part of the priapic orgies, and of which we have spoken before (p. 94). There women are presenting to him children, whom they have initiated in sorcery, and he shows them a deep pit, into which he threatens to throw them if they refuse to renounce God and to adore Satan.

In other parts are seen great cauldrons, full of toads and vipers, hearts of unbaptized children, flesh of criminals who had been hanged, and other disgusting ingredients, of which they make pots of ointments, &c. and poisons, the ordinary articles of commerce in this "fair." Of such objects, also, were composed the dishes served at the Sabbath tables, at which no salt was allowed, because Satan wished everything to be insipid, musty, and bad-tasted.

Here we see people " dancing, either ' in long,' in couples, turned back to back, or sometimes 'in round,' all turning their backs towards the centre of the dance, the girls and women each holding by the hand their demons, who teach them movements and gestures so lascivious and indecent that they would horrify the most shameless woman in the world; with songs of a composition so brutal, and in terms and words of such license and lubricity, that the eyes become troubled, the ears confounded, and the understanding bewitched, at the appearance of so many monstrous things all crowded together."

" The women and girls with whom the demons choose to have connection are covered with a cloud, to conceal the execrations and ordures attached to these scenes, and to prevent the compassion which others might have on the screams and sufferings of these poor wretches." In order to " mix impiety with the other abominations," they pretended to perform religious rites, which were a wild and contemptuous parody on the catholic mass. An altar was raised, and a priest consecrated and administered the host, but it was made of some disgusting substance, and the priest stood with his head downwards and his legs in the air, and with his back turned to the altar.

Thus all things were performed in monstrous or disgusting forms, so that Satan himself appeared almost ashamed of them.

De Lancre acknowledges that there was some diversity in the manner of the proceedings of the Sabbath in different countries, arising from difference in the character of the locality, in the " master " who presided, and in the various humours of those who attended. " But all well considered, there is a general agreement on the principal and most important of the more serious ceremonies. Wherefore, I will relate what we have learnt by our trials, and I will simply repeat what some notable witches deposed before us, as well as to the formalities of the Sabbath, as to all that was usually seen there, without changing or altering anything in what they deposed, in order that every one may select what he likes."

The first witness adduced by De Lancre is not one belonging to his own time, but dating back as far as the 18th of December, 1567, and he had obtained a copy of the confession. Estébene de Cambrue, of the parish of Amou, a woman twenty-five years of age, said that the great Sabbath was held four times a year, in derision of the four annual festivals of the Church. The little assemblies, which were held in the neighbourhood of the towns or parishes, were attended only by those of the locality; they were called "pastimes," and were held sometimes in one place and sometimes in another, and there they only danced and frolicked, for the devil did not come there in all his state as at the great assemblies. They were, in fact, the greater and lesser Priapeia. She said that the place of the grand convocation was generally called the " Lanne de Bouc " (the goat's heath), where they danced round a stone, which was planted in the said place, (perhaps one of the so-called Druidical monuments,) upon which was seated a great black man, whom they called " Monsieur." Each person present kissed this black man on the posteriors. She said that they were carried to that place on an animal which sometimes resembled a horse and at others a man, and they never rode on the animal more than four at a time. When arrived at the Sabbath, they denied God, the Virgin, " and the rest," and took Satan for their father and protector, and the she-devil for their mother. This witness described the making and sale of poisons. She said that she had seen at the Sabbath a notary, whose name she gave, whose business it was to denounce those who failed in attendance. When on their way to the Sabbath, however hard it might rain, they were never wet, provided they uttered the words, *Haut la coude, Quillet,* because then the tail of the beast on which they were mounted covered them so well that they were sheltered from the rain. When they had to make a long journey they said these words: *Pic suber hoeilhe, en ta la lane de bouc bien m' arrecoueille.*

A man seventy-three years of age, named Petri Daguerre, was brought before De Lancre and his fellow commissioners at Ustarits; two witnesses asserted that he held the office of master of ceremonies and governor of the Sabbath, and that the devil gave him a gilt staff, which he carried in his hand as a mark of authority, and arranged and directed the proceedings. He returned the staff to Satan at the close of the meeting.

One Leger Rivasseau confessed that he had been at the Sabbath twice without adoring the devil, or doing any of the things required from the others, because it was part of his bargain, for he had given the half of his left foot for the faculty of curing, and the right of being present at the Sabbath without further obligation. He said " that the Sabbath was held about midnight, at a meeting of cross roads, most frequently on the nights of Wednesday and Friday; that the devil chose in preference the stormiest nights, in order that the winds and troubled elements might carry their powders farther and more impetuously; that two notable devils presided at their Sabbaths, the great negro, whom they called Master Leonard, and another little devil, whom Master Leonard at times substituted in his place, and whom they called Master Jean Mullin; that they adored the grand master, and that, after having kissed his posteriors, there were about sixty of them dancing without dress, back to back, each with a great cat attached to the tail of his or her shirt, and that afterwards they danced naked; that this Master Leonard, taking the form of a black fox, hummed at the beginning a word ill articulated, after which they were all silent."

Some of the witches examined spoke of the delight with which they attended the Sabbath. Jeanne Dibasson, a woman twenty-nine years old, said that the Sabbath was the true Paradise, where there was far more pleasure than can be expressed; that those who went there found the time so short by reason of the pleasure and enjoyment, that they never left it without marvelous regret, so that they looked forward with infinite impatience to the next meeting.

Marie de la Ralde, "a very handsome woman tyenty-eight years of age," who had then abandoned her connection with the devil five or six years, gave a full account of her experience of the Sabbath. She said she had frequented the Sabbaths from the time she was ten years old, having been first taken there by Marissans, the wife of Sarrauch, and after her death the devil took her there himself. That the first time she was there she saw the devil in the shape of a trunk of a tree, without feet, but apparently sitting in a pulpit, with some form of a human face, very obscure; but since she had often seen him in man's form, sometimes red, sometimes black. That she had often seen him approach a hot iron to the children which were presented to him, but she did not know if he marked them with it. That she had never kissed him since she had arrived at the age of knowledge, and does not know whether she had kissed him before or not; but she had seen how, when one went to adore him, he presented sometimes his face to kiss, sometimes his posteriors, as it pleased him, and at his discretion. That she had a singular pleasure in going to the Sabbath, so that every time she was summoned to go there, she went as though it were to a wedding feast; not so much for the liberty and license they had there to have connection with each other (which out of modesty she said she had never done or seen done), but because the devil had so strong a hold on their hearts and wills that it hardly allowed any other desire to enter. Besides that the witches believe they are going to a place where there are a hundred thousand wonders and novelties to see, and where they hear so great a diversity of melodious instruments that they are ravished, and believe themselves to be in some terrestrial paradise. Moreover the devil persuades them that the fear of hell, which is so much apprehended, is a piece of folly, and gives them to understand that the eternal punishments will hurt them no more than a certain artificial fire which he causes them craftily to light, and then makes them pass through it and repass without hurt. And more, that they see there so many priests, their pastors, curés, vicars, and confessors, and other people of quality of all sorts, so many heads of families, and so many mistresses of the principal houses in the said country, so many people veiled, whom they considered to be grandees, because they concealed themselves and wished to be unknown, that they believed and took it for a very great honour and good fortune to be received there.

Marie d'Aspilcouëtte, a girl nineteen years old, who lived at Handaye, said that she had frequented the Sabbath ever since the age of seven, and that she was taken there the first time by Catherine de Moleres, who had since been executed to death for having caused a man's death by sorcery. She said that it was now two years since she had withdrawn from her relations with Satan. That the devil appeared in the form of a goat, having a tail and under it the face of a black man, which she was compelled to kiss, and that this posterior face has not the power of speech, but they were obliged to adore and kiss it. After-

PLATE XVI   THE WITCHES' SABBATH

OM DE LANCRE, 1613.

wards the said Moleres gave her seven toads to keep. That the said Moleres transported her through the air to the Sabbath, where she saw people dancing, with violins, trumpets, and tabors, which made a very great harmony. That in the said assemblies there was an extreme pleasure and enjoyment. That they made love in full liberty before all the world. That some were employed in cutting off the heads of toads, while others made poison of them; and that they made the poison at home as well as at the Sabbath.

After describing the different sorts of poisons prepared on these occasions, De Lancre proceeds to report the testimony of other witnesses to the details of the Sabbath. Jeannette de Belloc, called Atsoua, a damsel of twenty-four years of age, said that she had been made a witch in her childhood by a woman named Oylarchahar, who took her for the first time to the Sabbath, and there presented her to the devil; and after her death, Mary Martin, lady of the house of Adamechorena, took her place. About the month of February, 1609, Jeannette confessed to a priest who was the nephew of Madame Martin, who went to his aunt and merely enjoined her not to take the girl to the Sabbath any more. Jeannette said that at the solemn festivals all kissed the devil's posteriors except the notable witches, who kissed him in the face. According to her account, the children, at the age of two or three years, or as soon as they could speak, were made to renounce Jesus Christ the Virgin Mary, their baptism, &c. and from that moment they were taught to worship the devil. She described the Sabbath as resembling a fair, well supplied with all sorts of objects, in which some walked about in their own form, and others were transformed, she knew not how, into dogs, cats, asses, horses, pigs, and other animals. The little boys and girls kept the herds of the Sabbath, consisting of a world of toads near a stream, with small white rods, and were not allowed to approach the great mass of the witches; while others, of more advanced age, who were not objects of sufficient respect, were kept apart in a sort of apprenticeship, during which they were only allowed to look on at the proceedings of the others. Of these there were two sorts; some were veiled, to make the poorer classes believe that they were people of rank and distinction, and that they did not wish themselves to be known in such a place; others were uncovered, and openly danced, had sexual intercourse, made the poisons, and performed their other diabolical functions; and these were not allowed to approach so near " the master " as those who were veiled. The holy water used at the Sabbath was the devil's urine. She pointed out two of the accused whom she had seen at the Sabbath playing upon the tabor and the violin. She spoke of the numbers who were seen arriving and departing continually, the latter to do evil, the former to report what they had done. They went out at sea, even as far as Newfoundland, where their husbands and sons went to fish, in order to raise storms, and endanger their ships. This deponent spoke also of the fires at the Sabbath, into which the witches were thrown wtihout sustaining any hurt. She had seen the frequenters of the Sabbath make themselves appear as big as houses, but she had never seen them transform themselves into animals, although there were animals of different kinds running about at the Sabbath.

Jeanette d'Abadie, an inhabitant of Siboro, of the age of sixteen, said that she was taken for the first time to the Sabbath by a woman named Gratianne; that for the last nine months she had watched and done all she could to withdraw herself from this evil influence; that during the first three of these months, because she had watched at home by night, the devil carried her away to the Sabbath in open day; and during the other six, until the 16th of September, 1609, she had only gone to them twice, because she had watched, and still watches in the church; and that the last time she was there was the 13th of September, 1609, which she narrated in a "bizarre and very terrible manner." It appears that, having watched in the church of Siboro during the night between Saturday and Sunday, at daybreak she went to sleep at home, and, during the time of the grand mass, the devil came to her and snatched from her neck a "fig of leather which she wore there, as an infinity of other people did;" this *higo,* or fig, she described as "a form of hand, with the fist closed, and the thumb passed between the two fingers, which they believe to be, and wear as, a remedy against all enchantment and witchcraft; and, because the devil cannot bear this fist, she said that he did not dare to carry it away, but left it at the threshold of the door of the room in which she was sleeping." This Jeanette said, that the first time she went to the Sabbath she saw there the devil in the form of a man, black and hideous, with six horns on his head, and sometimes eight, and a great tail behind, one face in front and another at the back of the head, as they paint the god Janus. Gratianne, on presenting her, received as her reward a handful of gold; and then the child-victim was made to renounce her Creator, the Virgin, the baptism, father, mother, relatives, heaven, earth, and all that was in the world, and then she was required to kiss the fiend on the posteriors. The renunciation she was obliged to repeat every time she went to the Sabbath. She added that the devil often made her kiss his face, his navel, his member, and his posteriors. She had often seen the children of witches baptized at the Sabbath.

Another ceremony was that of baptizing toads. These animals perform a great part in these old popular orgies. At one of the Sabbaths, a lady danced with four toads on her person, one on each shoulder, and one on each wrist, the latter perched like hawks. Jeanette d'Abadie went on further in her revelations in regard to still more objectionable parts of the proceedings. She said that, with regard to their libidinous acts, she had seen the assembly intermix incestuously, and contrary to all order of nature, accusing even herself of having been robbed of her maidenhead by Satan, and of having been known an infinite number of times by a relation of hers, and by others, whoever would ask her. She always fought to avoid the embraces of the devil, because it caused her an extreme pain, and she added that what came from him was cold, and never produced pregnancy. Nobody ever became pregnant at the Sabbath. Away from the Sabbath, she never committed a fault, but in the Sabbath she took a marvellous pleasure in these acts of sexual intercourse, which she displayed by dwelling on the description of them with a minuteness of detail, and language of such obscenity, as would have drawn a blush from the most depraved woman in the world. She described also the tables

covered in appearance with provisions, which, however, proved either unsubstantial or of a disgusting
nature.

This witness further declared that she had seen at
the Sabbath a number of little demons without arms,
who were employed in kindling a great fire, into
which they threw the witches, who came out without
being burnt; and she had also seen the grand master
of the assembly throw himself into a fire, and remain
there until he was burnt to powder, which powder
was used by the witches to bewitch young children,
and cause them to go willingly to the Sabbath. She
had seen priests who were well-known, and gave the
names of some of them, performing the service of the
mass at the Sabbath, while the demons took their
places on the altar in the forms of saints. Sometimes
the devil pierced the left foot of a sorcerer under the
little toe, and drew blood, which he sucked, and after
this that individual could never be drawn to make
a confession; and she named, as an example, a priest
named Francois de Bideguaray, of Bordegaina, who,
in fact, could not be made to confess. She named
many other persons whom she had seen at the Sabbaths, and especially one named Anduitze, whose office it was to summon the witches and sorcerers to
the meeting.

De Lancre says that many others, in their depositions, spoke of the extreme pleasures and enjoyments experienced in these Sabbaths, which made men and women repair to them with the greatest eagerness. " The woman indulged before the face of her husband without suspicion or jealousy, he even frequently acted the part of procurer; the father deprived his daughter of her virginity without shame; the mother acted the same part towards her son; the brother towards his sister; fathers and mothers carried thither and presented their children."

The dances at the Sabbath were mostly indecent, including the well-known Sarabande, and the women danced in them sometimes in chemise, but much more frequently quite naked. They consisted especially in violent movements; and the devil often joined in them, taking the handsomest woman or girl for his partner. De Lancre's account of these dances is so minute and curious that it may be given in his own words. " If the saying is true that never woman or girl returned from the ball as chaste as she went there, how unclean must she return who has abandoned herself to the unfortunate design of going to the ball of the demons and evil spirits, who has danced in hand with them, who has kissed them obscenely, who has yielded herself to them as a prey, has adored them, and has even copulated with them? It is to be, in good earnest, inconstant and fickle; it is to be not only lewd, or even a shameless whore, but to be stark-mad, unworthy of the favours with which God loads her in bringing her into the world, and causing her to be born a Christian. We caused in several places the boys and girls to dance in the same fashion as they danced at the Sabbath, as much to deter them from such uncleanness, by convincing them to what a degree the most modest of these movements was filthy, vile, and unbecoming in a virtuous girl, as also because, when accused, the greater part of the witches, charged with having among other things danced in hand with the devil, and sometimes led the dance, denied it all, and said that the girls were deceived, and that they could not have known how to express the forms of dance which they said they had seen at the Sabbath. They were boys and girls of a fair age, who had already been in the way of salvation before our commission. In truth some of them were already quite out of it, and had gone no more to the Sabbath for some time; others were still struggling to escape, and, held still by one foot, slept in the church, confessed and communicated, in order to withdraw themselves entirely from Satan's claws. Now it is said that they dance always with their backs turned to the centre of the dance, which is the cause that the girls are so accustomed to carry their hands behind them in this round dance,

that they draw into it the whole body, and give it a
bend curved backwards, having their arms half
turned; so that most of them have the belly commonly great, pushed forward, and swollen, and a little in-
clining in front. I know not whether this be caused by
the dance or by the ordure and wretched provisions
they are made to eat. But the fact is, they dance very
seldom one by one, that is one man alone with one
woman or girl, as we do in our galliards; so they have
told and assured us, that they only danced there three
sorts of branles, or brawls, usually turning their
shoulders to one another, and the back of each looking towards the round of the dance, and the face
turned outwards. The first is the Bohemian dance,
for the wandering Bohemians are also half devils; I
mean those long-haired people without country, who
are neither Egytians (gipsies), nor of the kingdom of
Bohemia, but are born everywhere, as they pursue
their route, and pass countries, in the fields, and under the trees, and they go about dancing and playing
conjuring tricks, as at the Sabbath. So they are
numerous in the country of Labourd, on account of
the easy passage from Navarre and Spain.

" The second is with jumping, as our working men
practise in towns and villages, along the streets and
fields; and these two are in round. The third is also
with the back turned, but all holding together in

length, and, without disengaging hands, they approach so near as to touch, and meet back to back, a man with a woman; and at a certain cadence they push and strike together immodestly their two posteriors. And it was also told us that the devil, in his strange humours, did not cause them all to be placed in order, with their backs turned towards the crown of the dance, as is commonly said by everybody; but one having the back turned, and the other not, and so on to the end of the dance. . . . They dance to the sound of the tabor and flute, and sometimes with the long instrument they carry at the neck, and thence stretching to near the girdle, which they beat with a little stick; sometimes with a violin (fiddle). But these are not the only instruments of the Sabbath, for we have learnt from many of them that all sorts of instruments are seen there, with such harmony that there is no concert in the world to be compared to it."

Nothing is more remarkable than the sort of prurient curiosity with which these honest commissioners interrogated the witnesses as to the sexual peculiarities and capabilities of the demon, and the sort of satisfaction with which De Lancre reduces all this to writing. They all tend to show the identity of these orgies with those of the ancient worship of Priapus, who is undoubtedly figured in the Satan of the Sabbath. The young witch, Jeannette d'Abadie, told how she had seen at the Sabbath men and women in promiscuous intercourse, and how the devil arranged them in couples, in the most unnatural conjunctions—the daughter with the father, the mother with her son, the sister with the brother, the daughter-in-law with the father-in-law, the penitent with her confessor, without distinction of age, quality, or relationship, so that she confessed to having been known an infinity of times at the Sabath by a cousin-german of her mother, and by an infinite number of others. After repeating much that she had said before relating to the impudicity of the Sabbath, this girl said that she had been deflowered by the devil at the age of thirteen—twelve was the common age for this—that they never became pregnant, either by him or by any of the wizards of the Sabbath; that she had never felt anything come from the devil except the first time, when it was very cold, but that with the sorcerers it was as with other men. That the devil chose the handsomest of the women and girls for himself, and one he usually made his queen for the meeting. That they suffered extremely when he had intercourse with them, in consequence of his member being covered with scales like those of a fish. That when extended it was a yard long, but that it was usually twisted. Marie d'Aspilcuette, a girl between nineteen

and twenty years of age, who also confesesd to having
had frequent connection with Satan, described his
member as about half a yard long, and moderately
large. Marguerite, a girl of Sare, between sixteen
and seventeen, described it as resembling that of a
mule, and as being as long and thick as one's arm.
More on this subject the reader will find in De
Lancre's own text. The devil, we are further told,
preferred married women to girls, because there was
more sin in the connection, adultery being a greater
crime than simple fornication.

In order to give still more truthfulness to his account of the Sabbath, De Lancre caused all the facts
gathered from the confessions of his victims to be
embodied in a picture which illustrates the second
edition of his book, and which places the whole scene
before us so vividly that we have had it re-engraved
in facsimile as an illustration to the present essay.[1]
The different groups are, as will be seen, indicated by
capital letters. At A we have Satan in his gilt pulpit,
with five horns, the one in the middle lighted, for
the purpose of giving light to all the candles and
fires at the Sabbath. B is the queen of the Sabbath,
seated at his right hand, while another favorite,
though in less degree, sits on the other side. C, a
witch presenting a child which she has seduced. D,

---

[1] See our plate XVI.

---

the witches, each with her demon, seated at table. E, a party of four witches and sorcerers, who are only admitted as spectators, and are not allowed to approach the great ceremonies. F, " according to the old proverb, *Après la pance, vient la dance,*" the witches and their demons have risen from table, and are here engaged in one of the descriptions of dances mentioned above. G, the players on instruments, who furnish the music to which the witches dance. H, a troop of women and girls, who dance with their faces turned outwards from the round of the dance. I, the cauldron on the fire, to make all sorts of poisons and noxious compounds. K, during these proceedings, many witches are seen arriving at the Sabbath on staffs and broomsticks, and others on goats, bringing with them children to offer to Satan; others are departing from the Sabbath, carried through the air to the sea and distant parts, where they will raise storms and tempests. L, " the great lords and ladies and other rich and powerful people, who treat on the grand affairs of the Sabbath, where they appear veiled, and the women with masks, that they may remain always concealed and unknown." Lastly, at M, we see the young children, at some distance from the busy part of the ceremonies, taking charge of the toads.

In reviewing the extraordinary scenes which are

developed in these witch-depositions, we are struck
not only with their general resemblance among themselves, although told in different countries, but also
with the striking points of identity between the proceedings of the Sabbath. and the secret assemblies
with which the Templars were charged. We have in
both the initiatory presentation, the denial of Christ,
and the homage to the new master, sealed by the obscene kiss. This is just what might be expected. In
preserving secretly a religious worship after the open
practice of it had been proscribed, it would be natural, if not necessary, to require of the initiated a
strong denial of the new and intrusive faith, with
acts as well as words which compromised him entirely in what he was doing. The mass and weight
of the evidence certainly goes to prove that such
secret rites did prevail among the Templars, though it
is not equally evident that they prevailed throughout
the order; and the similarity of the revelations of
the witch-confessions, in all countries where they
were taken, seems to show that there was in them
also a foundation in truth. We look upon it as not
admitting of doubt, that the Priapic orgies and the
other periodical assemblies for worship of this description, which we have described in an earlier part
of this essay, were continued long after the fall of the
Roman power and the introduction of the Christian

religion. The rustic population, mostly servile, whose morals or private practices were little heeded by the other classes of society, might, in a country so thinly peopled, assemble by night in retired places without any fear of observation. There they perhaps indulged in Priapic rites, followed by the old Priapic orgies, which would become more and more debased in form, but through the effects of exciting potions, as described by Michelet,[1] would have become wilder than ever. They became, as Michelet describes them, the Saturnalia of the serf. The state of mind produced by these excitements would lead those who partook in them to believe easily in the actual presence of the beings they worshipped, who, according to the Church doctrines, were only so many devils. Hence arose the diabolical agency in the scene. Thus we easily obtain all the materials and all the incidents of the witches' Sabbath. Where this older worship was preserved among the middle or more elevated classes of society, who had other means of secrecy at their command, it would take a less vulgar form, and would show itself in the formation of concealed sects and societies, such as those of the different forms of Gnosticism, of the Stadingers, of the Templars, and

---

[1] See Michelet, *La Sorcière*, liv. i, c. 9, on the use and the effects of the Solaneæ, to which he attributes much of the delusions of the Sabbath.

---

of other less important secret clubs, of a more or less immoral character, which continued no doubt to exist long after what we call the middle ages had passed away. As we have before intimated, these mediæval practices prevailed most in Gaul and the South, where the influence of Roman manners and superstitions was greatest.

The worship of the reproductive organs as representing the fertilizing, protecting, and saving powers of nature, apart from these secret rites, prevailed universally, as we have traced it fully in the preceding pages, and we only recur to that part of the subject to state that perhaps the last traces of it now to be found in our islands is met with on the western shores of Ireland. Off the coast of Mayo, there is a small island named Inniskea, the inhabitants of which are a very primitive and uncultivated race, and which, although it takes its name from a female saint (it is the *insular sanctæ Geidhe* of the Hibernian hagiographers), does not contain a single Catholic priest. Its inhabitants, indeed, as we learn from an interesting communication to *Notes and Queries* by Sir J. Emerson Tennent,[1] are mere idolaters, and their idol, no doubt the representative of Priapus, is a long cylindrical stone, which they call *Neevougee*. This idol is kept wrapped in flannel, and is entrusted to

[1] *Notes and Queries*, for 1852, vol. v, p. 121.

the care of an old woman, who acts as the priestess. It is brought out and worshipped at certain periods, when storms disturb the fishing, by which chiefly the population of the island obtain a living, or at other times it is exposed for the purpose of raising storms which may cause wrecks to be thrown on the coast of the island. I am informed that the Name *Neevougee* is merely the plural of a word signifying a canoe, and it may perhaps have some reference to the calling of fishermen.

www.ingramcontent.com/pod-product-compliance
Lightning Source LLC
Chambersburg PA
CBHW020000290326
41935CB00007B/246